Kierkegaard's Critique
of Reason and Society

Kierkegaard's Critique of Reason and Society

Merold Westphal

THE PENNSYLVANIA STATE UNIVERSITY PRESS
University Park, Pennsylvania

Library of Congress Cataloging-in-Publication Data

Westphal, Merold.
    Kierkegaard's critique of reason and society / Merold Westphal.
        p.   cm.
    Originally published: Macon Ga. : Mercer University Press, © 1987.
    Includes bibliographical references and index.
    ISBN 0-271-00830-X (pbk. : alk. paper)
    1. Kierkegaard, Søren, 1813-1855. I. Title.
[B4377.W47   1992]   91-30516
198'.9—dc20   CIP

Contents

For Kirk and Karla
In gratitude
For the joy they have brought
And the fun they have been

Preface

It all began during one of my very first years as a teacher. I was all ready to give my first Kant seminar when the department chairperson called me in to see if I would be willing to do a seminar on Kierkegaard instead. There were any number of people in our department of nearly thirty who could give the Kant seminar, but it seemed no one else was both qualified and disposed to teach the melancholy Dane. I had done very little work on Kierkegaard and my primary qualification was only that I was disposed to offer such a seminar, though I haven't a clue how my deparment chairperson was able to anticipate that.

The seminar that ensued remains to this day the most exhilarating teaching experience I have ever had. (Essentially the same seminar, offered a year or two later, turned out to be the worst teaching experience I have ever had. I have long since given up trying to figure that out.) Not too long afterwards I was invited to give a lecture at the University of Virginia. I called that lecture "Kierkegaard and the Logic of Insanity." The written version of that lecture became the earliest of the essays collected in this volume.

Since that time I have taught Kierkegaard regularly, to graduate and undergraduate students, to seminary students, and even to noncredit students in a community-education program; and almost every other year I have written another essay on some aspect of his thought. While I have written more on Hegel, to whom my intellectual debts are enormous, it is Kierkegaard who has influenced my own thinking more than any other writer.

My first discovery was that the concepts of ideology and the sociology of knowledge were first worked out in the 1840s, not just by Marx but also by Kierkegaard. Since the terminology growing out of the Marxist tradition has become standard for talking about knowledge as social legitimation and the resulting dimensions of false consciousness involved in this, the presence of essentially the same discoveries in Kierkegaard has not been fully appreciated. The result of this, it increasingly seemed to me, was that Kierkegaard's critique of reason was all too frequently misinterpreted in "existentialist" and "irrationalist" terms. That the Reason before which Kierkegaard refused to bow down in worship was in his eyes an historically specific form of human deviousness was insufficiently noticed. Discovering the hermeneutics of suspicion and the critique of ideology in a thinker as passionately religious as Kierkegaard persuaded me that the fundamental insights of Marx, Nietzsche, and Freud were not the monopoly of atheistic unbelief. The idea of the religious philosopher in a prophetic mold began to emerge.

At the same time I was not comfortable with Kierkegaard's individualism. On the basis of Hegel, Marx, and, for that matter, the biblical prophets, it seemed to me that human existence was more fundamentally social than Kierkegaard's thought permitted. My second discovery was that the "individualist" interpretation was as fundamentally misleading as the "irrationalist" interpretation, reflecting more an a priori "existentialist" stereotype than a careful reading of the texts. Kierkegaard's individualism, I have become increasingly persuaded, expresses a radical politics and is anything but a form of apolitical or antisocial indifference or withdrawal.

It is around these two discoveries that all of the essays of this volume revolve. I make no claim to have been either the first or the only one to make these discoveries, though much discussion of Kierkegaard has been quite innocent of them. These discoveries are important to me not as events of scholarly history but as moments of personal illumination. Thus they are only secondarily discoveries *about* Kierkegaard. Primarily they are discoveries *through* Kierkegaard, insights gained with his help. I am delighted to be able to bring together in one place the essays that constitute this journey of discovery, partly because I believe they are genuinely unified around these two interrelated themes, but primarily because I can share what I have learned from Kierkegaard far more effectively in this way than through a series of scattered essays.

The essays are in thematic rather than chronological order. Chapter 1 serves in lieu of an introduction. It develops the concept of the philosopher of religion according to the model of the biblical prophet rather than that of the scientist (as expressed not only in the modern, experimental concept, but also in the concepts of *episteme* and *Wissenschaft*). Kierkegaard makes only cameo appearances in this essay, but in chapter 2 the concept is developed in detail with reference to his thought. Just as in the *Postscript* Kierkegaard develops the concepts of inwardness and subjectivity as the generic framework within which it is possible to address the more specific question of what it means to become a Christian, so I have first developed the general idea of the philosopher as prophet and then tried to show how its categories illuminate the writings of Kierkegaard.

It is clear from these first two essays that there are epistemological as well as ethical-political issues involved, and that the two types of issue are intimately interconnected. Chapters 3, 4, and 5 focus on the latter, developing Kierkegaard's social criticism, the major themes of which revolve around the amorality of modern society which simultaneously deifies, dehumanizes, and demonizes itself. Modern society deifies itself by taking itself to be the absolute point of reference both for itself and for its individual members. It dehumanizes itself by becoming mass society, a herd from which the individual in any ethically or religiously significant sense has been eliminated. The result is a demonic monster as powerful as it is unprincipled, the transcendental subject of what has become the age of nuclear terror.

The third of these essays, the one on Abraham and Hegel, brings the epistemological issue to the forefront. Its interpretation of the body of *Fear and Trembling* focuses on the problem of social self-deification. But its analysis of the frame within which the story of Abraham is retold focuses on the epistemic issues that are involved. Kierkegaard tries to show that Hegel's translation of religious ideas from the form of *Vorstellung* to *Begriff* is inseparable from the social self-deification he finds in Hegel's ethics.

The remaining essays explore Kierkegaard's theory of knowledge as an integral part of his prophetic social critique. Chapters 6 and 7 develop Kierkegaard's epistemology in terms of the sustained attention he gives to the sinful and social character of human reason and to the ideological character of its tendency to identify itself simply with Reason, as if the voice of the people were indeed the voice of God.

It might be thought that the essays on Kierkegaard as a social critic would derive primarily from his latest writings, especially his *Attack upon "Christendom."* But his prophetic dimension was no afterthought. I believe the latest writing referred to in these essays is from 1850. The texts dealt with most extensively are from the pens of Johannes de Silentio, Johannes Climacus, and Anti-Climacus, and thus from the very heart of Kierkegaard's authorship.

I have modified these essays slightly from the versions in which they originally appeared to give them a unity of form corresponding to the unity of content I believe they have always had. Grateful acknowledgment is given to the original publishers for permission to republish these essays in a single volume. The previous history of the essays is as follows.

"Prolegomena to Any Future Philosophy of Religion Which Will Be Able to Come Forth as Prophecy," *International Journal for Philosophy of Religion* 4:3 (Fall 1973).

"Kierkegaard as a Prophetic Philosopher," *Christian Scholar's Review* 7:2-3 (1977). First presented to the Twenty-Third Annual Wheaton College Philosophy Conference in October 1976.

"Kierkegaard's Politics," *Thought* 55:218 (September 1980; New York: Fordham University Press, copyright © 1980): 320-32.

"Kierkegaard's Sociology," in Robert L. Perkins, ed., *Two Ages,* International Kierkegaard Commentary 8 (Macon GA: Mercer University Press,1984).

"Abraham and Hegel," in Robert L. Perkins, ed., *Kierkegaard's Fear and Trembling: Critical Appraisals* (University AL: University of Alabama Press, 1981, 1983). Copyright © by University of Alabama Press.

"Kierkegaard and the Logic of Insanity," *Religious Studies* 7:3 (September 1971). Published by the Cambridge University Press. First given as a lecture at the University of Virginia.

"Inwardness and Ideology Critique in Kierkegaard's *Fragments* and *Postscript*," presented to the conference on Kierkegaard and Contemporary Philosophy at St. Olaf College, October 1985. Previously unpublished.

Abbreviations

CA   *The Concept of Anxiety,* vol. 8 of *Kierkegaard's Writings,* Reidar Thompte in collaboration with Albert B. Anderson, trans. (Princeton: Princeton University Press, 1980).

CI   *The Concept of Irony,* Lee Capel, trans. (New York: Harper & Row, 1965; Bloomington: Indiana University Press, 1968).

CUP   *Concluding Unscientific Postscript,* David F. Swenson and Walter Lowrie, trans. (Princeton: Princeton University Press, 1941).

EO   *Either/Or,* vol. 1: David F. Swenson and Lillian Marvin Swenson, trans.; vol. 2: Walter Lowrie, trans.; 2d ed.; rev. Howard A. Johnson (Princeton: Princeton University Press, 1971).

FSE   *For Self Examination* in *For Self Examination and Judge for Yourselves!,* Walter Lowrie, trans. (Princeton: Princeton University Press, 1941).

FT   *Fear and Trembling* in *Fear and Trembling/Repetition,* vol. 6 of *Kierkegaard's Writings,* Howard V. Hong and Edna H. Hong, eds. and trans. (Princeton: Princeton University Press, 1983).

JC   *Johannes Climacus* in *Philosophical Fragments / Johannes Climacus,* vol. 7 of *Kierkegaard's Writings,* Howard V. Hong and Edna H. Hong, eds. and trans. (Princeton: Princeton University Press, 1985).

JP   *Søren Kierkegaard's Journals and Papers,* 7 vols., Howard V. Hong and Edna H. Hong, assisted by Gregor Malantschuk, trans. (Bloomington: Indiana University Press, 1967-1978). Citations are by volume and *entry* number, not volume and page unless specifically noted.

OAR   *On Authority and Revelation, The Book on Adler,* Walter Lowrie, trans. (New York: Harper & Row, 1966).

PF   *Philosophical Fragments* in *Philosophical Fragments / Johannes Climacus*

PV   *The Point of View for My Work as an Author,* including "The Individual: Two 'Notes' Concerning My Work as an Author" and "My Activity as a Writer," Walter Lowrie, trans. (New York: Harper & Row, 1962).

SUD *The Sickness unto Death*, vol. 19 of *Kierkegaard's Writings*, Howard V. Hong and Edan H. Hong, eds. and trans. (Princeton: Princeton University Press, 1980).

SLW *Stages on Life's Way*, Walter Lowrie, trans. (New York: Schocken, 1967).

TA *Two Ages*, vol. 14 of *Kierkegaard's Writings*, Howard V. Hong and Edna H. Hong, eds. and trans. (Princeton: Princeton University Press, 1978).

TC *Training in Christianity*, Walter Lowrie, trans. (London and New York: Oxford University Press, 1941; rpt., Princeton: Princeton University Press, 1944).

WL *Works of Love*, Howard V. Hong and Edna H. Hong, trans. (New York: Harper & Row, 1964).

chapter

Prolegomena to Any Future Philosophy of Religion That Will Be Able to Come Forth as Prophecy

1

The question whether Kierkegaard is a philosopher is perhaps not as trivial as it seems. Those who read Kierkegaard for the substance of his writing are generally unconcerned about how he gets pigeon-holed. However, for others who regard themselves as philosophers and define their agenda in terms of contemporary professional discussion, the question is important. Where his thinking directly addresses contemporary issues it may be unavailable if he is *not* considered a philosopher. The result would be an impoverished philosophical discussion.

Since we are at what might be called the Kierkegaardian stage of the twentieth century, the time is ripe for putting aside doubts as to whether he is really a philosopher and for recognizing him not just as a historical figure who might be of interest to those who share his religious faith, but also as a full-fledged partner in the contemporary philosophical critique of reason and society.

It is not so outrageous to recognize the present as being a Kierkegaardian stage of twentieth-century philosophy. In one important respect, the twentieth century has recapitulated the nineteenth. Hegel developed the idea that philosophy must be scientific. Marx had radically different ideas about how to achieve this, but he remained faithful to the ideal. It was Kierkegaard who challenged the goal itself in what many consider his major work, *Concluding Unscientific Postscript.*

Twentieth-century philosophy has reenacted this scenario on two separate tracks. The revival of the ideal of scientific philosophy has been intimately linked to the concept of method. Husserl's ideal of "philosophy as rigorous science" became a seemingly endless task of spelling out the meaning of phenomenological method, and in the Anglo-American context the idea of philosophical analysis was to be the key.[1] These projects were vastly different, but throughout their many changes they maintained the idea of establishing scientific philosophy through the use of rigorous method, thus achieving an objectivity free from perspectival relativity. Philosophical rationality would embody, as Thomas Nagel appropriately puts it, *The View from Nowhere.*

In a very important sense Heidegger's *Being and Time* and Wittgenstein's *Philosophical Investigations* were the handwriting on the wall for these two attempts to restore philosophy to the dignity of science. But the disenchantment with the scientific ideal of philosophy has become considerably more radical since then. The paths that lead from Heidegger to Derrida and from Wittgenstein to Rorty[2] are what I call the Kierkegaardian stage of twentieth-century philosophy, the increasingly emphatic denial that philosophy can be or should try to be scientific. Kierkegaard should now be included as a full partner in contemporary philosophical discussion.

This essay seeks to facilitate his inclusion in two ways. First, it explores some of the difficulties with the idea of scientific philosophy in that branch of philosophy most closely associated with Kierkegaard in most people's minds, the philosophy of religion. One advantage that my procedure offers is a generalization of the issue by its removal from the specifics of Kierkegaard's satirical critique of Hegel. Second, it begins the development of an alternative model for philosophy. If philosophers should not think of themselves primarily in terms of the scientist, then perhaps the Hebrew prophet provides a better model. In the following chapter this possibility, developed here in general terms, will be explored with specific reference to Kierkegaard.

The prophetic model is not the only alternative. The sophist engages in "the perpetual life-and-death struggle of knowledge with the phenomenon in the service of egotism," or the service of freedom without responsibility.[3] Those who see the antiscientific mood of contemporary philosophy as inevitably culminating in nihilism are effectively saying that other than the scientist, the sophist is the only alternative model for the philosopher. If this is true, the development of a third model would be quite useful, but an understanding of why the scientific model is unsatisfactory and why alternative models need to be developed is the primary concern.

Until very recently the following account of the philosophy of religion was standard: philosophy of religion encompasses two activities, philosophizing about God and philosophizing about religion. The former represents the sus-

---

[1]Perhaps the best account of this is still that of J. O. Urmson, *Philosophical Analysis: Its Development between the Two World Wars* (Oxford: Clarendon Press, 1956).

[2]In one of the best philosophical ironies I recently found Reichenbach's *The Rise of Scientific Philosophy* immediately adjacent to Rorty's *Philosophy and the Mirror of Nature* on the shelves of the Hope College library.

[3]*CI*, 63.

tained life of natural theology and its negative correlate, natural atheology. They are concerned with proofs for the existence of God and related issues such as the problem of evil and the possibility of metaphysics. Philosophizing about religion, by contrast, has a subject matter whose reality is not in doubt. Religion is a plainly observable aspect of human experience. The philosophical task is to understand this phenomenon in its essence and manifestations. Hence this enterprise is often called the phenomenology of religion.

On closer examination it is impossible to distinguish these two species of philosophy of religion in terms of their subject matter. Natural (a)theology cannot avoid assertions that have a vital bearing on our understanding of religion as a human experience; and the phenomenology of religion devotes its attention to the object as well as to the subject of religion. One can, of course, distinguish the form and content of a mode of human experience such as religion from the putative object of that experience, which may be thought of as the cause of the experience or what is signified by the experience. In either case the immanence of this experience falls short of logically guaranteeing the transcendence of the object; and transcendence is understood as reached only through some form of mediation, inferential or interpretational. Apart from historical connections these considerations provide justification for defining these two modes of philosophy of religion as philosophizing about God and philosophizing about religion.

But they also help formulate this distinction more sharply, rendering the obvious overlap in subject matter less puzzling. Natural (a)theology is a normative enterprise that presents and evaluates arguments designed to establish the truth or falsity of religious assertions. Since religious assertions tend to be about God rather than religion, and since they tend to be most controversial where they surpass the immanence of experience, natural (a)theology can be easily described as philosophizing about God; but since assertions about religion often have a bearing on the truth or falsity of religious assertions, these too become the object of debate. A familiar example is the discussion of empirical verification and the meaning of religious language, which clearly belongs to the philosophy of religion as natural (a)theology.

The phenomenology of religion, however, is a descriptive enterprise. It is concerned with truth, but not with the truth of religious assertions; and it brackets questions of transcendence in order to describe the form and content of religion as an observable phenomenon. Phenomenology of religion discusses God, but it does so by describing various forms of belief in God rather than debating the truth of these beliefs. It is systematically uncommitted about the latter question.

Therefore the fundamental difference between natural (a)theology and phenomenology of religion is not that one is about God and the other about religion. Rather, one is normative and the other is descriptive. Further inquiry into the nature and purpose of the philosophy of religion would require that we ask what genus we have just divided into normative and descriptive species. The answer is probably not "rhetoric," "sophistry," "public relations," or "edification," but "science." Some respondents will be quite adamant about this answer; others will hesitate, even apologize. But even those who do not offer this answer and shy from its suggestion seem to have the idea in their subconscious. They are quite happy, for example, to write an article that is entirely noncommittal regarding the validity of the proof discussed (to say nothing of the larger question of God's reality). They are content to argue that, whatever one may want to say about the proof or the reality of God, it is clear that Professor P's objections to Professor R's formulations are not free from certain ambiguities, and in any case would not apply to all formulations of the proof. Would they find this a worthwhile activity if they had not been persuaded by Descartes that science progresses by dividing big questions into little questions and answering the little questions definitively, hoping subsequently to put the pieces together in answer to the big questions?

As we pursue our questioning we will notice that phenomenologists of religion will tend to be more confident than their natural (a)theological colleagues that their discipline is a science. Many will say that it is just because phenomenology is the one approach to religion that *can* be scientific that they engage in it. But even among the natural (a)theologians we are likely to find science running well ahead of any other well-defined alternative in our poll. As our Socratic task, we should examine the possibilities of natural (a)theology and phenomenology of religion being science, and this requires an agreement as to what we shall mean by science.

In order to keep the question both interesting and pertinent to our discussion, we shall steer clear of very narrow definitions. We certainly will not include the requirement of a measurable subject matter, and we should not insist on the formulation of general laws. Perhaps we can agree that the heart of science is objectivity. The scientist is the one who brackets all personal interests, values, and commitments that would have any bearing on his investigations. By a heroic act of self-renunciation he becomes the transcendental ego, a nonparticipating spectator. As such he is indistinguishable from other scientists, but the rewards for this sacrifice are based on just this fact. He presents his results to other scientists who are able to verify what is really there for the common transcendental ego and eliminate what is due to the residual idiosyncrasies of the original investigation. The result is acclaimed as universal truth. In this sense of intersubjective agreement one can speak of the public verification that renders scientific objectivity.

Can natural (a)theology be scientific in this sense? We are told that Hume and Kant have already been outflanked. Their critique of natural theology (and for Kant it applied with equal force to natural atheology) was that the modes of inference employed, where not inherently invalid as in the case of the ontological argument, cannot legitimately be extended to the question of God's existence. Furthermore, when illegitimately employed, they take their revenge by producing a being who comes conspicuously short of the glory of God. Both Hume and Kant assume, with some historical justification, that the modes of inference to be employed by natural theology are those used to establish those empirical uniformities that we call the laws of nature. Since the concept of general laws is excluded from our concept of science, we can concede to Hume and Kant their point, which is now of only historical interest, and proceed in the full awareness that one does not establish God's reality in the same way one confirms Newtonian mechanics.

Without waiting to be told what other modes of inference are to be employed, we must ask whether the heart of the Humean-Kantian critique does not in fact apply with different but equal force to the broader notion of scientific objectivity we are examining. The question is not whether scientific method can be applied legitimately to the question of God's existence but whether the scientific ideal is appropriate in this context. It seems that Kant's discovery of the a priori as the unconditioned condition of all possible experience touched off a whole series of discoveries showing many areas of thought where the a priori is radically conditioned by historical, sociological, and psychological factors. This indicates that the categories in which questions are framed and the principles by which answers are evaluated vary with the observer. Knowledge becomes radically perspectival and interest-bound.

Who can doubt that religion is such an area of thought? When the questions are about God and immortality—Where did I come from? Where am I going? What's it all about? Is it just for the moment we live?—is it not comical to speak of "pure *theoria*," the knower as "nonparticipating spectator" whose "fully disinterested seeing of the world" stems from "the *epoche* of all practical interests"?[4] The ideal of thought without the real thinker, the task of becoming the transcendental ego—what meaning can they have where thought is so fundamentally conditioned by the personal and collective life-worlds of the thinker?

It appears that the notion of scientific objectivity, even without the ideals of mathematical precision and general laws, when torn from its natural habitat and transferred to the religious realm reveals the fundamental incongruity between itself and its newly assigned subject matter. Kant and Hume were perhaps too specific in formulating the difficulty of rendering natural theology scientific. It is clear that the same difficulty applies to natural atheology. For example, when Freud psychoanalyzes belief in God in terms of the wish for continuing fatherly care during adult life and relegates arguments for God's reality to the realm of rationalizations, his own deep hatred of his father suddenly comes into focus as not unrelated, in terms of his own theory, to his own atheism. The insights of psychoanalysis move in both directions. Similarly, the scientific character of Marx's atheism is called into question by his own sociology of knowledge.

---

[4]These phrases are from Husserl's Vienna Lecture of 1935, translated as Appendix A in Edmund Husserl, *The Crisis of European Sciences and Transcendental Phenomenology*, David Carr, trans. (Evanston: Northwestern University Press, 1970).

Suppose these difficulties are ignored and natural (a)theology insists on being scientific. What will be the result? It will probably be rhetoric in the sense defined by Socrates in the *Gorgias* (459-465). Since objectivity expresses itself in public agreement, natural (a)theology will have to address itself to the crowd. But Socrates reminds us that "before *a crowd* means among the ignorant" and therefore there is "no need to know the truth about things but merely to discover a technique of persuasion, so as to appear among the ignorant to have more knowledge than the expert." What is the secret of this *technique* that generates the *appearance* of real knowledge? Simply that "it aims at what is pleasant, ignoring the good." This is to say it is like cookery, a form of flattery. Unlike medicine, which may, on the basis of its knowledge, prescribe what is good for the patient but most unpleasant, cookery simply wins favor by appealing to taste. Similarly, rhetoric, in order to win the agreement of the crowd and in this case give the appearance of being scientific, resorts to flattery by appealing to the preferences of the audience.

Since there are several communities of taste in religious matters, natural theologians seek out those with a taste for proving God while natural atheologians seek out those who would disprove him. They find their audiences and, after winning the acclaim of their followers, bask in the objectivity of their success. But don't go near them with Socratic questions unless you are prepared to discover that these transcendental egos can bite.

The pluralism extends further than this. Among those with a taste for proving the existence of God there are a variety of subgroups, including a mainstream natural theology and several sectarian varieties. Each of these is grounded in "Reason," but a close look at the deities produced reveals them as created in the image of the taste of communities that make each natural theology possible. And the same is true, *mutatis mutandis*, for natural atheology.

This is the heart of the crisis in the search for a scientific philosophy of religion. The phrases that I have quoted to help define the ideal of scientific objectivity are borrowed from Husserl's important Vienna Lecture of 1935, entitled "Philosophy and the Crisis of European Humanity." In it he asks why there is no applied science of the spirit corresponding to medicine, a science that could cure the European peoples of their desperate illness. The primary crisis is the spiritual condition of the national and supernational communities whose historical teleology Husserl traces from the Greek ideal of science. If a crisis in philosophy exists, it is its total incapacity to come forth as spiritual medicine. In calling his rhetoric an art, Gorgias viewed it as an applied science. But Socrates, after showing its affinity with cookery and not medicine, replies, "I refuse the name of art to anything irrational." I am asking the reader to seriously consider whether this is the same case with philosophy of religion as natural (a)theology.

At a time when the greatest religious upheaval since the Reformation is matched by national and international crises whose roots are plainly spiritual, does the philosophy of religion have any medical credentials? Are the sick waiting for a word from the transcendental ego? Is there any healing in words that point out that Professor P's objections to Professor R's formulations are not free from certain ambiguities and would not apply to all formulations of the proof? Do the communities of taste to which philosophers of religion resort really have something in common with a health spa? Or are the dainty dishes that they set before their kings real health foods?

This is the point at which phenomenologists argue that philosophy of religion can be a science. They have taken Kant seriously. They have heard him argue that metaphysics cannot be possible as a science in the transcendent sense, giving objective truth about God, freedom, and immortality; and they have also heard him explain that metaphysics can be possible as an immanent science describing the structures of human experience. This is the key to their withdrawal from normative to descriptive philosophy of religion. Instead of trying to bracket their religious interests, values, and commitments in order to discuss the truth of religious assertions objectively, they bracket the question of religious truth in order to describe religious phenomena objectively. Their work will constitute the Transcendental Analytic of the Critique of Pure Piety and set forth the categories and principles of religious experience, describing the life-world of faith.

This new knowledge is not completely disinterested. It is conditioned by an interest in being scientific. But perhaps this does not present the inherent obstacle to objectivity that religious interests have in discussions about God. While phenomenologists are not the "nonparticipating spectator" engaged in a "fully disinterested view of the world," it is possible to concede that they have achieved "the *epoche* of all practical interests."

However, even this may not be true. Part of the phenomenologists' motivation may be derived from a sense of the gulf between the God of the philosophers and the God of Abraham, Isaac, and Jacob. That is, they not only feel the difficulties that natural (a)theology has in being a science, but they recognize how far removed its questions are from the heart of actual religious concern. Instead of the abstract and remote God of the proofs, phenomenologists prefer to discuss the concrete and present God of the believer. They are familiar with the experience of Anselm, who, after proving God's existence beyond reasonable doubt, cried out in anguish because he did not experience what he had proved. They "would be happy to sacrifice the 'must be' of rational dialectic in exchange for the 'is' of encounter."[5]

Now phenomenologists know that talking about the believer's putative encounter with God is not the same as encountering God; but it is hard to escape the impression that they often think of it as somehow closer to encountering God than is all the discussion about the existence of a prime

---

[5]I owe this formulation to John Smith, who also called my attention to the experience of Anselm. See his "How Can We Speak of Experiencing God?" *The Journal of Religion* 50 (1970): 234-35.

mover. In short, I am suggesting that one of the interests underlying phenomenology of religion is a religious interest. This is why phenomenology looks suspiciously like an indirect form of natural theology, slipping from the description of religious experience to an argument from religious experience.

These two paths into phenomenology of religion correspond to the twofold critique by Hume and Kant of natural (a)theology. The scientific interest that directs a move from normative to descriptive corresponds to their questions about the inferences employed, while the religious interest that directs a move from the abstract and metaphysical to the concrete and experiential corresponds to their questions about the religious value of the proofs, regardless of validity. But now it appears that the interests that have responded to these insights may not be compatible. If there are religious interests underlying the phenomenology of religion, then "the *epoche* of all practical interests" may not have been achieved, and the bracketing of the question of religious truth may have been more apparent than real. It is one thing to articulate a methodology, another to practice it. Perhaps even the phenomenology of religion cannot be a science.

Nietzsche once said that Homer would not have created Achilles, nor Goethe Faust, if Homer had been an Achilles or Goethe a Faust. His point was simply that being a hero and being a heroic poet are mutually exclusive capacities. A similar relation seems to obtain between scientific and religious interests. Since this would have a bearing on the scientific status of phenomenology of religion, assuming that my previous suggestions are correct, I wish to raise a somewhat different question. For this purpose it will be helpful to illustrate the contrast more carefully.

First, we can juxtapose quotations from Kant and Barth. The former said of the founders of the scientific revolution, Galileo et al., "They learned that reason has insight only into that which it produces after a plan of its own, and that it must not allow itself to be kept, as it were, in nature's leading strings, but must itself show the way . . . constraining nature to give answers to questions of reason's own determining." If metaphysics would find the "sure road to science" it must undergo just such a Copernican revolution. "Hitherto it has been assumed that all our knowledge must conform to objects. . . . [Instead, let us] suppose that objects must conform to our knowledge."[6]

And Barth:

God's revelation in its objective reality is the incarnation of His Word. . . . It becomes the object of our knowledge; it finds a way of becoming the content of our experience and our thought; it gives itself to be apprehended by our contemplation and our categories. But it does that beyond the range of what we regard as possible for our contemplation and perception, beyond the confines of our experience and thought. . . . It becomes the object of our knowledge by its own power and not by ours. . . . We can understand the possibility of [this knowing] solely

---

[6]*Critique of Pure Reason,* B xiii-xv.

from the side of its object, i.e., we can regard it not as ours, but as one coming to us, imparted to us, gifted to us. In this bit of knowing we are not the masters but the mastered. . . . Knowledge in this case means acknowledgement. And the utterance or expression of this knowledge is termed confession.[7]

The difference here is too plain to need comment. It will be even more vivid if we think of Job. The first Job we meet is the Kantian Job. "God," he says, "where are you? I've got some questions for you. I really think you ought to show up." But after the encounter, in which God does show up, only a Barthian Job remains. In the presence of the majesty of God, his questions no longer seem so important, and he is suddenly aware of his own limitations.

> *I have uttered what I did not understand,*
> 　　*things too wonderful for me,*
> 　　*which I did not know.*
> *"Hear, and I will speak;*
> 　　*I will question you, and you declare to me."*
> *I had heard of thee by the hearing of the ear,*
> 　　*but now my eyes see thee;*
> *therefore I despise myself,*
> 　　*and repent in dust and ashes.*
> 　　　　(Job 42:3-6)

In place of the "questions of reason's own determining," we find only acknowledgement and confession.

Next we can compare Aristotle and Socrates as philosophers of religion. In the opening pages of *Metaphysics,* Book Alpha, Aristotle tells us about the science that is divine, not only because it is fit for God to engage in but also because it has God as its object. It is founded in wonder, which he interprets as sheer intellectual curiosity, the desire for knowledge, for its own sake. Hence it is historically subsequent to those sciences that concern either our pleasure or our necessities. Since it is obviously a luxury, it first appears and continues to reside among the leisure class.

For Socrates, by contrast, philosophy is not born of idle curiosity, but in the experience of the cave. The awareness of the darkness and captivity in which one dwells makes it a desperate pursuit for light and freedom. This is the same experience, Shestov reminds us, to which the Psalmist refers when he says, "Out of the depths I cried unto Thee, O Lord."[8] If the philosopher seems a bothersome bore (gadfly) to others, he is only seeking to come to grips with mortality, preparing for death. Far from being an act of leisure, this pursuit is so necessary that it does not allow Socrates the time to attend to his business affairs. Perhaps this is why, when one speaks disparagingly of the God of phi-

---

[7]*Church Dogmatics,* Bromily and Torrance, eds. (Edinburgh: T. & T. Clark, 1956) 1:2:172-73.

[8]See the foreword to Lev Shestov, *Athens and Jerusalem,* Bernard Martin, trans. (New York: Simon and Schuster, 1968).

losophers, one thinks of Aristotle, but not of Socrates. Socrates' God is more like the God of Abraham. He would have embraced the passage from Barth with joy. (One can almost see him standing rapt for hours reading about "The Miracle of Christmas," "The Revelation of God as the Abolition of Religion," etc.). Aristotle would have gone away shaking his head, totally perplexed at the way such nonsense could be written by someone fortunate enough to have lived after Kant.

If Aristotle and Kant see *science* as the exercise of human power directed toward the mastery of its object while Socrates and Barth view *religion* as the experience of desperate need alleviated only by some gift of grace, then Kierkegaard focuses on another aspect of the difference between the two when he tells us that "sin does not properly belong in any science. It is the theme with which the sermon deals, where the individual talks as an individual to the individual."[9] Because of the differences already alluded to, the objectivity proper to science is improper in relation to religious subject matter, in this case sin. To talk about sin is to talk about what concerns individuals in all their subjectivity. Sin has no relation to the transcendental ego. One can be sure that when one raises only the "questions of reason's own determining," the topic will not come up; it is equally unlikely that the leisure class will ever have enough leisure to get curious about sin. This is why, from the religious point of view, truth cannot be found in objectivity.

Since these contrasts between scientific and religious points of view raise troublesome questions about the phenomenology of religion, one is not entirely prepared to find them so clearly summarized as they are in the opening paragraph of a classic in that discipline, van der Leeuw's *Religion in Essence and Manifestation.*

> That which those sciences concerned with Religion regard as the *Object* of Religion is, for Religion itself, the active and primary Agent in the situation or, in this sense of the term, the *Subject.* In other words, the religious man perceives that which his religion deals as primal, as originative or causal; and only to reflective thought does this become the Object of the experience that is contemplated. For Religion, then, God is the active Agent in relation to man, while the sciences in question can concern themselves only with the activity of man in his relation to God; of the acts of God himself they can give no account whatever.[10]

At first glance this is nothing but the disclaimer by which the phenomenologist moves to the descriptive in order to be scientific; but if we recall that our reflections on differences between the scientific and religious stances were triggered by Nietzsche's suggestion that Homer could not have written the *Iliad* if he had been an Achilles, a question arises. If van der Leeuw had been

[9] *CA,* 16. Cf. *FSE,* 64, where the only shame to be felt in the world where science reigns is that of being truly subjective.

[10] G. van der Leeuw, *Religion in Essence and Manifestation,* J. E. Turner, trans. (New York: Harper & Row, 1963) 1:23.

a man of faith, could he have written his classic work? The question is obviously not whether a particular individual professes to be a religious believer in some sense, nor is it even a question whether a person with religious interests could write a scientific phenomenology of religion. The question is whether it would be appropriate to try.

The sort of tension that leads to this question does not exist between natural science and the philosophy of science. The same pursuit of detached objectivity is fundamental to both. However, between religion and a scientific philosophy of religion no such harmony exists. Instead it appears that the phenomenology of religion can be justified only in terms of interests that are foreign, even hostile, to the subject matter. Whether a discipline with such a discrepancy between methodology and subject matter could still be called scientific is a question I will leave to whomever is interested. My concern is whether such a discipline can serve as spiritual medicine in the crises of our time. While it is clear, in terms of van der Leeuw's distinction, that the truth about "the acts of God himself" would have a bearing on our spiritual health, can the same be said about an objective description of "the activity of man in his relation to God"?

A thinker like Husserl can be optimistic here because he sees our civilization as having its teleological essence in the scientific ideal of the Greeks (and one might add—of the Greeks *qua* Aristotle, not *qua* Socrates). This being so, the health of our civilization is nothing other than the health of our science. But our civilization has its roots in biblical religion as well; and when this is realized Husserl's analogy between physical and spiritual medicine as applied sciences will lose its obviousness. What reason do we have to think that a scientific phenomenology of religion (assuming it to be possible in some sense) would have any healing words to address to the specifically religious crisis of our time, since it has so assiduously cut itself off from religious involvement in order to give us disinterested descriptions? Can it give a patient in need of medicine anything more than a pharmaceutical a la carte? What spiritual guidance can it give to the larger national and international crises of the day? Can its typology of religious structures discern whether religion is a reproach to any people or whether it exalts a nation; or whether some types of religion serve the one purpose and others the other? In short, is there any sense at all in speaking about the application of this science? Perhaps Aristotle was right: a scientific philosophy of religion is a luxury.

These considerations are by no means the last word on the subject of a scientific philosophy of religion, but they may make it easier to explore the possibility that the model for a philosopher of religion can be someone other than a scientist. There are numerous interesting possibilities, but I shall consider only one, the Hebrew prophet. Like apostles, prophets are distinguished from geniuses in that their message is presented on divine authority. The listener is asked to accept the message not because of its profundity, eloquence, or beauty, but because "thus saith the Lord." Mindful of Kierkegaard's insistence that he spoke without authority, I do not wish to suggest that philosophers of religion seek to imitate prophets in this respect. The upshot of my thinking is not to propose a kerygmatic philosophy of religion that is indistinguishable from preaching. There are other characteristics of prophetic speech that philosophers of religion might well seek to imitate. I have in mind particularly its character as *personal, untimely, political,* and *eschatological.*

To say that prophetic speech is personal is to say that, unlike scientific discourse, it comes in the mode of direct address. This is because it echoes God's address to human hearers. For example,

> *I am the Lord your God, who brought you out of the land*
> *of Egypt, out of the house of bondage.*
> *You shall have no other gods before me.*
> (Ex. 20:2-3)

A particular person is addressing a specific audience in a particular situation. In such speech monotheism is not a theoretical hypothesis for discussion, e.g., Resolved: there are no other Gods but Yahweh. "Israel is told that it is *forbidden* for other gods to exist. Forbidden that *they* should have other gods; but it only concerns *them,* who are addressed, and the whole reality of the subject under discussion is that of the relation between YHVH and Israel."[11]

Thus it never occurs to the prophets to present their message in the mode of universally valid truths and imperatives. Nor do they take a scientific stance toward their message as phenomenologists of the word of the Lord. That word has come to them too personally and directly for them to treat it objectively. "We shall be disappointed if we imagine that . . . the prophets give a complete account of the phenomenology of the word of Yahweh. Indeed, we may even come to think that the prophets are the last people to provide an answer to this question, because their attitude to the word they receive is so far from neutral. . . . In his word Yahweh meets his prophet in the most personal way possible; how could a man then talk of it as if it were a neutral thing?"[12]

This is why the prophets bring *the* word of the Lord, not *a* word. God's word is not a bundle of timeless, universally valid propositions, as Lessing thought, one or two of which are periodically presented for our listening pleasure. What He says at a particular time to a particular audience is the only word that matters, hence *the* word of the Lord.

Prophetic speech reflects this character of personal address even where it does not come prefaced by "thus saith the Lord." Kierkegaard knew this and although he repeatedly insisted that he spoke "without authority," he always addressed himself to "that single individual" who might find edification in what he wrote. While he occasionally means Regina by this phrase, it usually refers to the one he so often addresses as "my dear reader." This explains why he

[11]Martin Buber, *The Prophetic Faith* (New York: Harper & Row, 1960).

[12]Gerhard von Rad, *Old Testament Theology,* D. M. G. Stalker, trans. (New York: Harper & Row, 1962-1965) 2:80, 88-89.

should pause in a treatise on the phenomenology of anxiety to remind us that "sin does not properly belong in any science. It is the theme with which the sermon deals, where the individual talks as an individual to the individual." The phenomenology of anxiety is everywhere subordinated to the task of invoking in the reader a holy dread, not of evil in the world, but of his or her own sin. The author is not a transcendental ego, nor his reader a nonparticipating spectator. Rather Kierkegaard has sought to hear God's truth in a personal way and then pass it on, albeit without authority, in an equally personal way.

It is not surprising that this is precisely the alternative that Socrates chose over Gorgias's rhetoric. While discussing the tyrant Archelaus and his thesis that it is better to suffer wrong than to do it, he is met by Polus's scornful and ironic reply, "And I suppose there are other Athenians besides yourself who would prefer to be any Macedonian rather than Archelaus." He replies that while this method of appealing to many witnesses is effective in the law courts, it is "worthless toward discovering the truth." Then Socrates pointedly tells how he became a laughingstock while presiding at a meeting of the Council because he did not know how to put the question to a vote, indicating that what is best for people cannot be decided by ballot. Instead "I know how to produce one witness to the truth of what I say, the man with whom I am debating, but the others I ignore. I know how to secure one man's vote, but with the many I will not even enter into discussion" (471-474).

This personal character of prophetic speech accounts for the tendency of prophetic argument to be *ad hominem*. For example, Amos does not provide a formally valid proof from universally self-evident premises that Yahweh is a faithful God; nor does he deduce from pure reason the imperative to be faithful to Him. Instead he says

> *Seek good, and not evil,*
> *   that you may live;*
> *and so the Lord the God of hosts,*
> *   will be with you,*
> *   as you have said.*
> (Amos 5:14)

The premise of his argument is his hearers' profession that Yahweh is their God and they are His people.

A more contemporary example of the same *ad hominem* argument might look like this.

> *I have read the* Reader's Digest
> *from cover to cover*
> *and noted the close identification*
> *of the United States and the Promised Land*
> *where every coin is marked*
> *In God We Trust*

> *but the dollar bills do not have it*
> *being gods unto themselves.* [13]

In these lines Ferlinghetti does not prove that God alone is God and that Mammon is an idol. He simply challenges us either to worship God alone or to take "In God We Trust" off our coins and explicitly abandon our profession of being a Christian nation. Nor does he challenge the American Ideal. He asks us either to make a more serious and sacrificial effort at realizing the ideal or to recognize the *Reader's Digest*'s identification of the United States with the Promised Land for the idolatry it now is. Like Jonah, he is so far from presenting universal and necessary truths that he gives us a message that we ourselves can falsify if we repent. And with more prophetic spirit than Jonah, he pleads with us to do so.

Of course, since these are not necessary truths, they are not universally prophetic. The audience is important. Addressed to the dropouts of American society, these potentially prophetic words become mere flattery. But addressed to those who claim to live in the Promised Land and who tend to confuse "In God We Trust" with "In U.S. God Trusts," these words have the first mark of prophetic speech, personal address expressed in *ad hominem* argument.

They also illustrate the second characteristic of prophetic speech, its untimeliness. Prophetic speech is conspicuously out of step with the spirit of its times. It is always the speech of a minority, even when addressed to sectarian minorities. Hence it is lonely speech from the viewpoint of the speaker, while from the perspective of the hearer it is simply untimely and unwelcome. Its negations do not harmonize with the prevailing *nomos* into which prophetic speech injects itself. In the light of this *anomie* it should come as no surprise that Hosea was thought a fool and a madman by his hearers (Hos. 9:7).

In the Soviet Union this idea is taken seriously, and untimely meditations are often rewarded with confinement in a mental institution. We Americans are somewhat more subtle about it, but if we cannot escape the "thou art the man" addressed to us in "The Grand Inquisitor" by remembering that Dostoyevski had Catholicism in mind, we take comfort in remembering that the extremeness of his ideas is no doubt attributable to his epilepsy; just as we take comfort in knowing that the authors of *Attack upon Christendom* and *The Anti-Christ* were not mentally stable.

The untimeliness of prophetic speech is grounded in its distinctive view of the law of God, a view to be distinguished from the covenantal and pharisaical views. The covenantal view sees the law as the gift of grace to guide the covenant people through the wilderness of life. It is particularly prevalent in the Psalms.

---

[13]Lawrence Ferlinghetti, *A Coney Island of the Mind* (New York: New Directions, 1958) 63.

Oh, how I love thy law!
   It is my meditation all the day . . .
Thy word is a lamp to my feet
   and a light to my path.
                                        (Ps. 119:97,105)

It is easy to slip from this view to the pharisaical view that sees the law as security. Its mere possession provides a kind of magical claim on God's favor. This is the view Jeremiah faced, when he said,

I have given heed and listened,
   but they have not spoken aright;
no man repents of his wickedness
   saying, "What have I done?"
Everyone turns to his own course,
   like a horse plunging headlong into battle.
. . . my people know not
   the ordinance of the Lord.
How can you say, "We are wise,
   and the law of the Lord is with us?"
But, behold, the false pen of the scribes
   has made it into a lie.
                                        (Jer. 8:6-8)

It is characteristic of the prophets that while they attack the traditions in which the people rest, they are more deeply rooted in those traditions than the people who find their security in them. They are untimely just because they take so seriously what their contemporaries take for granted. Thus they do not deny the covenantal view of the law; but they do remember that the covenant contained both blessings and curses. Because they take the covenant so seriously, they recite not only the *Heilsgeschichte,* the story of God's saving acts, but also the *Unheilsgeschichte,* the story of Israel's ungrateful and rebellious response. In this context there is no ground for seeing the law as security; and it is not enough to see the law as a gift of grace. It is necessary to view the law as judgment, threat, wrath, and curse.[14] The untimely message of the prophets is that God's holy war is no longer directed against our enemies but against ourselves, His people. No wonder priest and king see the prophet as a conspirator, the one telling the other that "the land is not able to bear all his words" (Amos 7:10).

There is, of course, no guarantee that the untimeliness of prophetic speech will not be a vehicle for the prophets' personal resentments. They, willing to justify themselves, may be all too happy in their speeches to thank God publicly that they are not like others. This means that the *how* as well as the *to whom* is crucial to prophetic speech. Genuine prophetic speech contains the

---

[14]For a cogent argument that the prophetic view of the law as threat was not new but implicit in the original covenant, see Walter Zimmerli, *The Law and the Prophets,* R. E. Clements, trans. (New York: Harper & Row, 1967).

reluctance, not of Jonah, but of Jeremiah, who feels himself to be a vessel into which God's wrath is poured. As a mediator between God and his people, he shares both in the agony of his God whose love has turned to wrath and in the anguish of his people when they feel the foundations of their world shaken.

In speaking of the personal and untimely character of prophetic speech it has not been possible to avoid foreshadowing its political character. This lies at the heart of the prophetic mission to unfold the political nature of the question of God's existence. This is manifest in the confrontation between prophet and king throughout Hebrew monarchy. The presupposition of this relationship is that the whole of national life is subordinate to the will of God. The immediate corollary of this is that kingship represents delegated authority responsible to God. This is in striking contrast to the surrounding nations who sacralize their politics, not by subjecting it to the will of God, but by deifying the king, making him the incarnate presence of the head of the pantheon and thus an absolute authority.

At first, in the persons of Samuel, Nathan, and Elijah, the prophets' untimely words to the king concern his personal sins and the fate of his dynasty; but increasingly, as is the case with Amos, the conflict with the king grows out of a message of judgment on the nation as a people, of whom the king is but the actual and symbolic head. To see this message as political is to see that it does not only condemn idolatry but also the social injustices that undercut the solidarity of the social fabric and the secularism that seeks to found the national life on military strength and foreign alliances.

Why then should it be the priest who runs to the king to denounce Amos? Because Amos denounces the official cult as well as the social evils of his day. But in the prophetic view the former is not simply the responsibility of the priest and the latter that of the king. Rather the two represent a kind of conspiracy to limit Yahweh's sphere of influence. If the priest helps to identify the realm of divine concern with cultic activity, then the king's politics can be free of the yoke of the Torah. Not only can he tolerate the social injustices on which his courtiers and vassals thrive, but he can play the international geopolitical game with other kings free of entangling alliances with Yahweh.

In this case the cult can hardly be the true worship of Yahweh, and the idolatry implicit in the king's secularism will surely win out in the sacred realm as well. So it is not correct to say that prophets protest against both the religious and social sins of the people. The two are inseparable, and the prophetic opposition to priest and king is an opposition to the whole dualism of sacred and secular that they represent. It is the call to a religion that functions seven days a week and to a politics whose piety is more visible in policy than in church attendance.[15]

---

[15]For this view of the prophetic opposition to priest and king, see Buber, *The Prophetic Faith,* 67-95, and von Rad, *Old Testament Theology,* 2:39.

Jeremiah, who is perhaps best known for protesting the attempt to sustain the nation by an alliance with Egypt, knew the kind of religious atmosphere in which such a policy could be popular. So he went to the temple and said,

> Thus says the Lord of hosts, the God of Israel, Amend your ways and your doings, and I will let you dwell in this place. Do not trust in these deceptive words: "This is the temple of the Lord, the temple of the Lord, the temple of the Lord." For if you truly amend your ways and your doings, if you truly execute justice one with another, if you do not oppress the alien, the fatherless or the widow, or shed innocent blood in this place, and if you do not go after other gods to your own hurt, then I will let you dwell in this place. . . . Will you steal, murder, commit adultery, swear falsely, burn incense to Baal, and go after other gods that you have not known, and then come and stand before me in this house, which is called by my name, and say "We are delivered!" - only to go on doing all these abominations? Has this house which is called by my name, become a den of robbers in your eyes? Behold, I myself have seen it, says the Lord. (Jer. 7: 3-7, 9-11)

Finally, in turning to the eschatological character of prophetic speech, we note that the untimely words of the prophet are not only reluctant and anguished, but also penultimate. Prophetic preaching of the law is followed by the prophetic gospel. Good news is possible only because the prophetic view of time not only denies the sufficiency of the past and the ultimacy of the present, but also affirms the priority of God's future.

The prophets deny the continuing validity of the old institutions, sacred and secular, of the nation. But if their anomic announcements rob the people of their (false) security and create an intolerable terror and anxiety, it is not from sheer delight in destruction, but to prepare the way of the Lord.[16] They anticipate a new order in which God's very presence obliterates the gulf between sacred and secular. They see the history of salvation as continuing (since God is not dead), and thus they look forward to a whole new era of saving acts: a new exodus and covenant, accompanied by a new Moses; a new life for a spiritually dead people, and a new heart with which to serve the Lord; a new entry into the land, a new David, a new Zion, and a new temple.

In this way the unbridgeable gulf between Yahweh and the other gods is made clear. Those gods were once-upon-a-time gods; they were present to their people only in cultic reenactment of primordial acts recounted in cosmogonic myths. It is true that Hebrews turned to historical rather than mythological deeds, but a god who is not now doing something toward a future that is his is still a once-upon-a-time god, a fairy tale. And so Jeremiah called his people away from Sinai to a new covenant, as Isaiah called them from the exodus to a new deliverance through the wilderness, and as Ezekiel called them from bemoaning the loss of their temple to faith in the God who just might build a new one.

---

[16]Perhaps this is the point where the prophetic model differs most sharply from the sophistic model. Thus Kierkegaard represents a different kind of negation from the decenterings of radical deconstruction.

The difference is not just that God is absent in a new direction, future rather than past. The crux of the prophetic eschatology comes in its view of the present. By interpreting the present in terms of the future instead of the past, it becomes possible to see the present in bold new ways. Instead of seeing change as an aberration in a fixed order due to bad luck or poor strategy, it becomes possible to see it as the harbinger of new saving acts that God is about to perform. This makes it possible to prepare for God's future instead of being overwhelmed by it.

Now let us suppose that philosophers of religion, bringing to bear all of their special training and skills, were to address their contemporaries in this personal, untimely, political, and eschatological manner.[17] It is difficult to predict the result, and even harder to tell whether there would be any healing in it. Clearly it would be a bitter pill, and hard to swallow, but then medicine often comes in that form. Perhaps there would be some healing in the kind of philosophy that took Amos and Jeremiah as models rather than Galileo and Newton. And perhaps the best way to explore this possibility further would be to look more closely at that philosopher who, more than any other since Socrates, does this kind of philosophy—Soren Kierkegaard.

---

[17]This essay has its own ironic history. In its original form it was written by invitation for a symposium volume, but the editors who originally requested it found it too untimely and decided not to have their names associated with it.

Kierkegaard as a Prophetic Philosopher

2

In conversation with an able and distinguished philosopher from a Christian college, well known for the excellence of its philosophy department, I confided that I had been doing some work on Kierkegaard. "I went through a Kierkegaard stage once," he replied, "as an undergraduate."

I think I know what he meant. I recall the New York City student who told me of his precocious, intellectual group of high school friends. Unless you were led by Camus to the verge of suicide by your fifteenth birthday, you just weren't part of the gang. And I can recall the German students for whom Nietzsche played a similar role, leading them into their mid-teens with an ironically Cartesian certainty that God is dead, everything is permitted, and nothing matters. There is no doubt something about every writer who gains the existentialist label, even if he be Christian, which panders to just those prejudices that make adolescence something to be outgrown.

So I can understand how Kierkegaard might be perceived as a stage on life's way, and an undergraduate stage at that. In other words, there are real dangers involved in teaching Kierkegaard to undergraduates; and to teach him responsibly is to discover what these dangers are in any given situation and to take precautions against them. I would even mention Hegel's powerful critiques of the subjectivism of his day as among the most edifying sources of reflection on this problem.[1]

But I do not wish to dismiss Kierkegaard on the grounds that he is dangerous. For I find him to be dangerous in another way that we *cannot* do without. Just as faith is, on his analysis, a second immediacy after reflection, so there is a second reading of Kierkegaard that comes after adolescence. He himself suggests that his thought is most relevant after the identity crises of youth have passed.[2] It is when a man or woman has married, chosen a vocation and set-

---

[1] In addition to the famous preface to the *Phenomenology,* see the first half-dozen of the *Lectures on the Proofs for the Existence of God* and the discussion of Jacobi in *Faith and Knowledge.*

[2] *CUP*, 78ff.

tled down to the life that Judge William so passionately treasures that the question of subjectivity and seriousness should be posed.

What is that indispensable dangerousness that a second, postadolescent reading of Kierkegaard might reveal? The clue is revealed in reading Kierkegaard as a prophetic philosopher and taking seriously the suggestion to view Kierkegaard as a kind of paradigm of this alternative to philosophy as science. In the previous chapter, prophetic speech has been characterized as being personal, untimely, political, and eschatological. There can be no doubt that Kierkegaard's sustained attack upon Christendom is prophetic in these terms. But it may be claimed that it is not properly philosophical. There may be those who grant that Christendom needs its prophets, but argue that this is not the philosopher's task. My reply is fourfold.

First, we need to beware of too tight a disciplinary division of labor. For, while good fences make good neighbors (even in the academy), they do not necessarily make good thinkers, especially where integration and the unity of truth are clichés that we try to take seriously. We must be suspicious of boundaries when they become merely simplistic rationalizations. We do not wish to imitate those who distinguish the roles of prophet and evangelist so sharply that the evangelist is always welcome at the palace.

Second, we need to be aware of Marx, Nietzsche, and Freud. Even convinced theists cannot dismiss the critiques of established religion presented by these men on the grounds that they are atheists. They expose the Christendom of our day with the same scathing suspicion that Jeremiah and Amos directed against the Judaism of their day. Since the church usually has not provided its own prophets, the mantle of prophecy has fallen to the Babylonians and Assyrians. The church may be getting the rebuke it deserves from these secular prophets, but many outside the faith are misled into drawing conclusions about God that do not follow from the faithlessness of his people, and this is a tragedy.

Isn't it better to hear the painful truth about God's people from those who are compelled to tell it by their faithfulness to God, rather than from those who would like to do away with Him in the name of truth? And would it not be better still if such faithful prophets could draw on the conceptual power that accompanies philosophically acute thinkers such as Marx, Nietzsche, and Freud?

Third, modern philosophers are not the only ones who have taken up the prophetic task of subjecting popular religion to critical scrutiny. We are duly awed by the graceful way in which philosophy blends with theology and apologetics in the work of thinkers such as Augustine, Anselm, and Aquinas. An even more ancient tradition, represented by Xenophanes, Plato, and Plotinus, more closely parallels the prophets.

Since the repudiation of popular anthropomorphism by Xenophanes and Plato is grounded in an appeal to moral values that are undermined by the Olympian theology, one could say that, like the secular prophets of our day, they seek to oppose the moral point of view to the religious to the clear detriment of the latter. But this would not be correct because in either case the motivations are not secular, even those of a secular morality. Both thinkers, Plato perhaps more clearly, are critical of a prevailing religious establishment because of their commitment to what they believe to be a better affirmation of the divine; they teach us that there are pious as well as impious motives for protesting the creation of God in our own image. The same can be said of Plotinus's critique of the gnostic sects; it is not grounded in secular enlightenment, but in a deeply felt and carefully reasoned theology.

Do not these thinkers provide a historical precedent and something of a model for the notion of prophetic philosophy? To say so does not suggest that speculation must correct the gospel. Like Kierkegaard in the face of Lessing and Hegel, the Christian thinker must protest against this whenever it is found. But the Christian thinker has, again like Kierkegaard, both the right and the duty to seek an understanding of the faith and subject Christendom to critical evaluation on the basis of that understanding. Once more like Kierkegaard, it is wise to grant that this is done without authority. The prophetic philosopher cannot be confused with the prophet, whose "thus saith the Lord" is not part of the model.

Finally, let us look directly at Kierkegaard's attack upon Christendom. It is so thoroughly entwined with philosophical issues that no competent discussion of it could occur in a philosophical vacuum. Unfortunately, philosophers often do this by dismissing Kierkegaard as an irrationalist without carefully analyzing the arguments that resulted in his Lutheran comments about reason. These philosophers fail to notice how deeply rooted these arguments are in the sociology of knowledge.

If the indispensable danger of Kierkegaard *for us* is his prophetic critique of Christendom, we must take note of slogans he uses to express that critique and inquire into the particulars hidden behind them. Kierkegaard tells us that "Christendom has abolished Christianity," which it has "smuggled out of the world." Consequently, "one must try again to introduce Christianity into Christendom."[3] Incarnation, which is the heart of true Christianity, is "at variance with (human) reason" and thus offensive to the degree that Christ can only be the object of faith if he is at once the sign of offense.[4] This variance and offense stem from the fact that faith requires one to be contemporaneous with Christ and, more specifically, with Christ in his humiliation and not his glory—for no one is offended by glory.[5] Like Nietzsche, who claims that no one has understood his *Zarathustra* "who has not at some time been profoundly wounded and at some time profoundly delighted by every word of it," Kierkegaard complains that a Christianity that has suppressed the offense is

_____

[3] *TC*, 109, 104, 39.

[4] Ibid., 28.

[5] Ibid., 69.

"a superficial something which neither wounds nor heals profoundly enough."
More than being merely useless, it is idolatry, a "false invention of human
sympathy," or, as Xenophanes and Plato would have put it, the creation of
God in our own image.[6]

Kierkegaard supports this indictment with a bill of particulars that falls into
two general categories, the epistemological and the ethical facets of the offense involved in contemporaneity with Christ. These take the form of Kierkegaard's assault on apologetics and on a life-style rooted in the established
order.

Kierkegaard suggests that the man who fell among thieves on the road from
Jerusalem to Jericho did not suffer as much as Christianity will in the hands
of its apologists, since the latter want to do what the enemies of Christian faith
hope to do, which is to make Christianity reasonable.[7] With friends like that,
he suggests, who needs enemies? Then, as if fearing we might miss the point,
he proceeds to describe the inventor of the notion of defending Christianity
in Christendom as Judas No. 2 and the attempt to develop historically
grounded apologetics as blasphemy.[8] Perhaps we are beginning to get a notion of how the priests felt when they saw Jeremiah or Amos coming to the
temple.

Underlying Kierkegaard's verdict on apologetics is a sophisticated philosophical skepticism that deserves careful scrutiny.[9] It includes the Kantian
theme of the finitude of human reason vis-à-vis the Unconditioned and the
Pauline and Reformed theme of the sinfulness of human reason vis-à-vis a
holy God. Both can be part of an ahistorical view of human reason. But Kierkegaard goes beyond this to a recognition that human reason is a social enterprise and, as such, historically conditioned. This is where the genuinely
prophetic element becomes apparent. When the finitude and sinfulness of
human reason are included in reason's historicity, the critique of reason becomes a critique of ideology and Kierkegaard becomes more than just another skeptic, doubtful about the soundness of apologetic arguments. He is
persuaded that the final result will be corrupted Christianity, that the failure
of apologetics lies not so much in an inability to provide the demonstrations
or plausibilities it promises as in making promises that lead in the wrong direction altogether. How so?

Without any help from Marx, Nietzsche, Durkheim, Weber, or Scheler (but
with a lot from Hegel), Kierkegaard is sensitive to the sociology of knowledge. He knows that social groups make themselves legitimate through the

---

[6]Ibid., 139. Nietzsche's comment is from the preface to *The Genealogy of Morals.*

[7]*OAR,* 60.

[8]*SUD,* 87 and *TC,* 32ff.

[9]For more detailed discussion of the epistemological issues, see "Kierkegaard and
the Logic of Insanity," ch. 6 below.

propagation of belief systems in which the established order is justified. He also knows that religions are usually the most effective institutions in the practice of this "world-building" and "world-maintaining" function.[10] He recognizes (and this is crucial) the degree to which this process determines what is to count as Reason in any given context.

Consider the unforgettable response of the clergyman who is first projected into contemporaneity with Christ and then called upon for his verdict. He concedes that though all are looking for the Expected One, no *"reasonable man"* will take Jesus to be that One. For "the world development is . . . evolutionary not revolutionary. The veritable Expected One will therefore appear totally different; He will come as the most glorious flower and the highest unfolding of the established order. . . . He will recognize the established order as an authority."[11] For him reason is man's capacity to recognize the authority of the established order, thereby participating in its self-deification. When this is what masquerades as Reason, Kierkegaard asks why we should pledge allegiance to it. Where Reason means putting the question of truth to majority vote, as the clergyman goes on to suggest Jesus should do, has one not the right and duty to speak of Reason as Luther spoke of the Pope? Surely the public has become a greater menace than the Pope, on Luther's view, a fact not changed by calling its opinion Reason.[12] Reason has become treason against God. That "the established order is the rational" becomes a tautology and "use and wont become articles of faith." This is "the constant rebellion, the permanent revolt against God." Does not every established order, just like every individual, need to stand in fear and trembling before God?[13]

At this point we may be sitting like David prior to Nathan's statement "Thou art the man." We are indignant at all of this and quite confident that those engaged in it should be exposed, like the awful clergyman in Kierkegaard's thought experiment. Though it would have been a bit more honest of him to use his upper case E's and O's on "established order" rather than on "Expected One," he was candid enough about his rejection of Christ. Lord, I thank thee that we are not like that rascal, that we do not reject you or take the name of reason thus in vain.

Kierkegaard begs our pardon for not joining in our spontaneous doxology. He has learned that there is more than one way to reject Christ. There is Lessing's way, which openly confesses offense and, in the name of Reason, leaves the incarnation aside as unbelievable and unbelieved. Such was Kierkegaard's clergyman. But there is also Hegel's way, which purports to affirm the

---

[10]These are the terms used by Peter Berger in *The Sacred Canopy,* a valuable aid to understanding Kierkegaard on this point.

[11]*TC,* 50. My italics.

[12]*FSE,* 40.

[13]*TC,* 86-95.

incarnation and assign the highest rational expression to it, but does so in terms of a Reason that is the authoritative voice of the established order and that therefore distorts the gospel out of recognition. Lord, I thank thee that we are not Hegelians.

Kierkegaard again begs our pardon for not being in a doxological mood. He has learned that there is more than one way to be a Hegelian. The crucial question here is not whether our affirmation of the incarnation is orthodox or (like Hegel's affirmation)heretical. The question is what kind of established order our apologetics legitimates. The answer to this question determines whether our appeals to Reason are Hegelian or not, whether Reason is a name we use to obscure our creation of God in our own image to serve as the cosmic validator of our institutions and life-styles. Because the *content* of ideas does not provide any clearly defined limits on their *use*,[14] orthodoxy is no guarantee against this form of idolatry. Kierkegaard, in fact, is not at all sure it's possible to keep the arguments for Christianity's reasonableness from being heard as affirmations of Christendom's righteousness.

In this way there arises that which in Kantian language is called the priority of practical over theoretical reason. The epistemological question becomes part of the larger ethical question—apologetics as a question of discipleship. It becomes necessary to say that "faith is against understanding" because "faith is on the other side of death," the death that dies to immediacy, selfishness, and worldliness.[15]

This is to say that the offense of contemporaneity with Christ means not just that the socially sanctioned reasonableness of belief is rendered questionable, but also that the socially sanctioned rightness of behavior is rendered suspect. Like Socrates, Christ was executed as an infidel because he refused to recognize the established order as the criterion of virtue and goodness. In this sense Christ was an offense even without claiming godhead. He showed "what 'the truth' had to suffer in every generation and what it must always suffer" by not retreating from the collision between piety and the established order.[16]

But even in that assumption of divine status that sets him off so sharply from Socrates, only half of the offense lies in the fact that an individual man takes himself to be God (an offense of loftiness or exaltation, as Kierkegaard calls it). The other part exists in Christ's presentation of himself as God without acting like God, but living in a condition of humiliation rather than of glory (an offense of lowliness).

In the long run even the masses turn against him on this ground. Who wants a king whose investiture is symbolized by a manger, a towel, and a cross—

---

[14]Karl Mannheim makes this point most clearly in *Ideology and Utopia.*

[15]*FSE*, 101. See n. 19 below for Kierkegaard's view of worldliness.

[16]*TC*, 87, 37.

who, moreover, calls his own to follow in the same narrow way?[17] To say that it requires "a most frightful act of decision for a man to become a Christian" and that "only the consciousness of sin can force one into this dreadful situation" is to do more than simply note the logical leap involved in affirming what cannot be demonstrated, that this man is God.[18] We must recognize that one makes that leap—if it is indeed the leap of true faith and not a poor substitute—[19] not blindly, but in the full awareness that the One who is the Way and the Life and the Truth lived the life of a poor, suffering, impotent outcast through his identification with the poor, the suffering, and the impotent people on the fringes of his own society.[20] Is that any way for God to act among us?

Why does he not teach us to sing that the church *triumphant* is alive and well.[21] Why does he offer us the prize of contemporaneity with himself and then dash our hopes and insist that we should be contemporary with his humiliation where this life is concerned? Was it fair for him to stage a resurrection in such a way that the most discerning of the disciples were bound to greet the news with a barely stifled, "Oh no. Not him again!"[22] Why should respectable people like Nicodemus have to visit him in secret and at night, as if he were a prostitute?

By emphasizing the inevitability of these questions Kierkegaard has, as some would put it, quit preachin' and gone to meddlin'. Less colloquially, we might say that he is taking his general thesis about the relation between the ethical and the religious, familiar from the *Fear and Trembling* version of the Abraham story,[23] and drawing it closer to home. The requirement of faith is that the follower should become contemporary with Christ in his humiliation. This does not mean sacrificing Isaac, an illustration quite remote from our situation. What, then, does it mean?

In *Training in Christianity* much of Kierkegaard's answer comes in his meditation on Jesus' invitation, "Come hither to me, all ye that labour and are

---

[17]Ibid., 108-109; *FSE,* 64. These are the contexts in which Kierkegaard is apt to say that Christianity is not a doctrine, not merely a theoretical matter without practical implications.

[18]*TC,* 100, 71.

[19]*FSE,* 40-41. This passage makes it clear that "worldliness" for Kierkegaard means what "cheap grace" means for Bonhoeffer.

[20]At *TC,* 105 the offense of lowliness is defined in terms of these characteristics. For examples of what Kierkegaard has in mind, see 16, 40-41, 45-47, 52-53, 58, 61-63, 90, 111, 115-17; and *FSE,* 43, 47, and 77-87.

[21]*TC,* 90, 109.

[22]I owe this suggestion to an Easter sermon of Rev. William Sloan Coffin, Jr.

[23]For a more detailed interpretation, see "Abraham and Hegel," ch. 5 below.

heavy laden, I will give you rest." Consider just two motifs from this meditation. First:

> "Come hither to me!"—Wonderful! For human compassion does indeed do
> something for them that labour and are heavy laden. One feeds the hungry, clothes
> the naked, gives alms. . . . But to invite them to come to us, that is a thing that
> cannot be done; it would involve a change in all our household and manner of
> life. *It is not possible while one is living in abundance,* or at least in joy and glad-
> ness, to live and dwell together in the same house, in a common life and in daily
> intercourse, with the poor and wretched, with them that labour and are heavy
> laden. In order to be able to invite them thus one must live entirely in the same
> way, as poor as the poorest.[24]

As newcomers to town we received a lay couple's invitation to visit their
church. The church is located near the largest concentrations of minority
population in the area, which in this case happens to be Latino. We asked
whether there was any substantial Latino representation in the congregation
and were told that there was, so far as they knew, only one couple. On reflection they thought that perhaps only the husband was Latino. We did not
ask why. There was a brief pause in the conversation. Then they said, "It's
quite an affluent church."

The ethical tells us to be generous out of our abundance, whereas the religious, understood as contemporaneity with Christ, makes a more radical
demand.[25] The former is a reasonable demand; the latter is a bit extreme, if
not absurd. Generosity is a virtue, whereas identification with the poor is
probably the result of an unstable personality, if not outright madness.[26]
Or again:

> "Come hither." . . . He does but one thing, He opens his arms. He will not first
> (as righteous people do, alas, even when they are willing to help), He will not
> first ask thee, "Art thou not after all to blame for thy misfortune? Hast thou in fact
> no cause for self-reproach?" . . . Oh, it is such an exquisite invention of cruel
> pleasure, to enhance the consciousness of one's own righteousness in contrast
> with a sufferer, by explaining that his suffering is God's condign punishment. . . .
> He will not be thy benefactor in so cruel a fashion.[27]

To become contemporary with Christ is to give up that "cruel pleasure" that,
as Nietzsche also reminds us, is reinforced by morality. No doubt this movement is a necessary condition for the prior movement, for it is only as we cease
to judge the poor and oppressed that we are able to begin sharing in their suffering. But it is not a sufficient condition, at least if my experience is any mea-

---

[24]*TC,* 12. My italics.

[25]Compare the critique of "false generosity" in Friere's *Pedagogy of the Oppressed.*

[26]For a vivid portrayal of the point see George Mavrodes, "The Salvation of Zachary
Baumkletterer," *The Other Side* 12:1 (1976): 12ff.

[27]*TC,* 19-20.

sure. Progress in giving up the cruel pleasure of moral superiority is both easier and much quicker than movement toward the limitless abandon of divine compassion—"to make oneself literally one with the most miserable."[28]

In Kierkegaard's analysis, Reason, the ethical, and the established order become indistinguishable. But "as against God we are always in the wrong."[29] So if the Reason to which we appeal in our social and political thought is the authoritative voice of an established order that has made it difficult for Christians to hear the requirements of discipleship clearly, Kierkegaard will call for a dose of the absurd and the irrational in our social ethics. He will surely be misunderstood in doing so—by those who find it more convenient not to get his point. And if our apologetics legitimates this established order by approving a Christianity that lives at peace with it, Kierkegaard will call for a moratorium on apologetics. He will challenge us to go and learn what it means to be contemporary with Christ in His humiliation and then return to apologetics, unless we find that true discipleship leaves us no energy for apologetics or reveals a better apologetics than what we are familiar with.

My final comment is a simple, logical point for the benefit of myself and all who are more delighted than wounded by what I've said. Kierkegaard thinks that "the serious Christian might well find the whole situation of established Christendom in the highest degree offensive."[30] It is tempting to conclude that offense at established Christendom indicates a serious Christian. Logicians call this "the fallacy of affirming the consequent."

---

[28]Ibid., 63.

[29]From the sermon at the end of *Either/Or*.

[30]*TC*, 114.

Kierkegaard's Politics

3

In one of his earliest writings, *The Soliloquies,* Augustine carries on the following dialogue with Reason:

A. I desire to know God and the soul.
R. Nothing more?
A. Nothing whatever.

In this brief exchange, as in the better-known *Confessions,* the intensity of the individual's direct relation to God is such that the world tends to fade from view entirely. It is as if in the prayer that opens *The Soliloquies* Augustine had been overwhelmed by the question, "What shall it profit a man if he gain the whole world and lose his own soul?," and in response was willing to resign all interest in the world of nature and history.

According to the prevailing understanding of Kierkegaard's authorship, he is the modern heir and propagator par excellence of this dimension of Augustinian spirituality. In opposition to the worldly philosophy of bourgeois society and the philosophical worldliness of Hegelian speculation, his radical, religious individualism focuses all but exclusive attention on the self in its lonely confrontation with God.

The most vivid representative of this heroic piety is Abraham, so alone with God that he cannot communicate with either Isaac, his son, or Sarah, his wife, about what he is doing; he is so passionately committed to God that he is willing to renounce his highest earthly joy and violate his highest earthly duty to serve Him.

Continuing with this view, the *Concluding Unscientific Postscript* and *Sickness unto Death* are even more abstract, philosophical expressions of the earlier poetical images of *Fear and Trembling.* The *Postscript* is explicit that the worlds of nature and history pale into triviality before the passionately interested subjectivity of the existing individual. "[God] is in the Creation, and present everywhere in it, but directly He is not there; and only when the individual turns to his inner self, and hence only in the inwardness of self-ac-

tivity, does he have his attention aroused, and is enabled to see God."[1]
"Therefore, says the ethical, dare, dare to renounce everything, including this
loftily pretentious and yet delusive intercourse with world historical contemplation, dare to become nothing at all, to become a particular individual, of
whom God requires everything."[2]

In like fashion *Sickness unto Death* defines faith as follows: "By relating
itself to its own self and by willing to be itself, the self is grounded transpar-
ently in the Power which constituted it."[3] In other words, the highest human
potentiality is to be a responsibly self-determining self-consciousness before
God. Once again, God and the soul encounter each other on a stage so dimly
lit that it is invisible.

In the context of this reading of Kierkegaard, an essay on his politics could
only be a biographical commentary on his sympathy for monarchy and his
distaste for the revolutionary fervor of 1848. It could not be an interpretation
of his authorship, for as a writer he had no politics. In Hegelian language, he
has a philosophy of absolute spirit, art, religion, and philosophy, but no philosophy of objective spirit. He does write about marriage, but he never gets beyond this to a politics proper or a theory of economic and political institutions.
Furthermore, he no sooner posits marriage as an ethical task than he demands that we transcend this ethical domain and leap to a religious sphere
of existence whose paradigm, already noted, is Abraham, lonely and world-
less.

There are abundant data to support this reading of Kierkegaard; the reading
would not be so widespread if there were not. But there are abundant data in
support of the thesis that the earth is flat. In the present case I believe the data
are misinterpreted, largely through a failure to notice how deeply Hegelian Kierkegaard is on two points. A proper recognition of these points will enable us to
discover not only a politics in Kierkegaard's writings, but one with considerable
contemporary relevance.

The first point concerns Kierkegaard's individualism. It is not a reversion
to the individualism that Hegel's understanding of spirit protests. The latter
is analytic or compositional individualism, the view that complex wholes are
made up of preexisting, self-sufficient parts. This view was expressed in at
least three forms during the seventeenth and eighteenth centuries.

Descartes' use of geometrical proof as a model of the analytic method of
reasoning is the first. In such a proof, a series of simple inference units are
added together, each building on earlier steps but independent of the proof's
conclusion. The conclusion is so complex that it lacks the obviousness that
each step possesses. Just as buildings that can't be lifted are built of bricks

---

[1]*CUP*, 218.

[2]Ibid., 133.

[3]*SUD*, 131.

that can be lifted, so complex conclusions lacking self-evidence are established by simple steps that do possess self-evidence.

The empiricists developed an epistemology and psychology with the same structure. Our complex ideas are composed of simple ideas that become associated in accordance with discoverable laws, and our character and behavior are expressions of the sum total of environmental influences upon us. To evaluate our knowledge claims and to control our behavior we must analyze complex patterns in terms of the simple building blocks that compose them. Twentieth-century sense-data theory and behaviorist psychology are the heirs of this empiricism.

A third pre-Hegelian form of compositional individualism underlies social-contract political theory. The idea of society or the state as a voluntary association of presocial or prepolitical individuals presupposes, as in the other two cases, that the parts that make up a whole are independent of that participation. Inclusion in the whole is an optional or accidental relation into which they enter, but it is not part of their essential identity.[4] The colleague who tells me he views the state as an insurance company, to be judged simply in terms of providing benefits at reasonable costs, expresses this point of view perfectly. My relationship to my insurance company is no part of my essential identity.

Hegel's philosophy renounces compositional individualism and all its works. This is clear in the definition of spirit he gives in his first book, *The Phenomenology of Spirit*. He calls spirit, the distinguishing mark of human experience, "this absolute substance which is the unity of the different independent self-consciousnesses which, in their opposition, enjoy perfect freedom and independence: 'I' that is 'We' and 'We' that is 'I.' "[5]

Spirit is the I that is We. As the I it is personal self-consciousness. But it is always already more than that, for it always already says We as well as I. To say that the I is We is to say that it is essentially relational. Who am I? I am who I myself am *and* I am who We are. There may be groups to which I belong that are no part of my essential identity, but there are always groups that are. Conspicuous among these, in Hegel's view, are my family, my language community, and my country. I am who I am largely by being one of us Westphals, one of us English speakers, and one of us Americans. We should not think of this as an addition to who I myself am. It is I myself who am what I am largely by being one of various Us-es.

The second half of Hegel's formula for spirit is a bit ambiguous. It points out that the We is itself an I, while it also reminds us that the individuals who

---

[4]Rousseau makes a decisive break with compositional individualism but inconsistently clings to the contract metaphor. I especially have Hobbes and Locke in mind here.

[5]G. W. F. Hegel, *The Phenomenology of Spirit*, trans. A. V. Miller (Oxford: Clarendon Press, 1977) 110.

constitute the We are not absorbed into it without remainder but remain the dispersed centers in which spirit lives. The We is not only an I; it is also many I's. It has a collective identity, personality, and self-consciousness, while simultaneously being the interaction of distinct individuals. Both ways in which spirit is the We that is I are familiar to us, Hegel would insist, in our everyday experience of the family.

This conception of spirit represents a complete break with compositional individualism by *denying,* at least for central aspects of human experience, the existence of the kind of individuals it postulates—I's that do not already essentially say We—and by *affirming* the existence of social wholes having a life of their own that cannot be reduced to the sum of contributions of their various members.

It is equally important to note that this conception of spirit expresses an individualism of its own; for it emphasizes the *I* that is We and insists that the We remains dispersed in a plurality of *I's.* Hegel seems especially eager to stress this dialectical individualism. He writes, in the passage quoted above, that spirit "is the unity of the *different independent self-consciousnesses* which, in their *opposition,* enjoy perfect freedom and *independence*" (my italics).

The first step toward understanding Kierkegaard's politics is to recognize that he shares with Hegel this conception of spirit and the dialectical individualism contained therein. Being dialectical, this individualism is a social theory of human experience, inherently political in a broad sense. Kierkegaard's task, as he sees it, is to rescue this theory of what it is to be human, and its corresponding practice, from a Hegelian philosophy that is insufficiently faithful to it and from a society of which Hegel's philosophy is an all too faithful expression.

The second important Hegelian element in Kierkegaard's politics is the dialectical manner in which he defends dialectical individualism. He practices the negative dialectic of Hegel's *Phenomenology of Spirit* in which consciousness is led to its positive affirmations not through the dogmatic assertion of a position, since "one bare assurance is worth just as much as another,"[6] but rather through the determinate negation of positions that cannot survive the critical scrutiny of being compared to their own, self-imposed standards.

To emphasize the radically threatening force of a philosophy grounded in "the tremendous power of the negative," Hegel describes it as a "way of despair" and a kind of violent, spiritual death.[7] "But the life of spirit is not the life that shrinks from death and keeps itself untouched by devastation, but rather the life that endures it and maintains itself in it. It wins its truth only when, in utter dismemberment, it finds itself. It is this power, not as something positive, which closes its eyes to the negative. . . . On the contrary, spirit

---

[6]Ibid., 49.

[7]Ibid., 19, 49-52.

is this power only by looking the negative in the face, and tarrying with it. This tarrying with the negative is the magical power that converts it into being."[8] This flamboyant rhetoric implies the simple idea that we discover philosophical truth indirectly, by exposing philosophical error.

This is only one dimension of what Kierkegaard means by indirect communication, but his readers will have little trouble recognizing a genuinely Hegelian appreciation of the power of negative thinking behind his infatuation with irony and satire.

We should not be surprised, then, if Kierkegaard's politics is more like Marx's than Plato's in its form—if it emerges indirectly, through a critique of what he believes is the overriding sociopolitical defect of the theory and practice of his times rather than as a positive description of the institutions of the society he deems most rational.

The parallel with Marx is only formal. Kierkegaard, though writing in the same decade during which Marx worked out the essentials of his own views, does not take capitalism to be the besetting sin of his times any more than he takes atheism to be an essential ingredient in human fulfillment. His diagnosis centers on a lack of subjectivity, the failure of people to be passionately committed, ethicoreligious individuals.

But the individualism he wishes to evoke is neither compositional individualism, to put it philosophically, nor bourgeois individualism, to put it sociopolitically. It is actually the dialectical individualism he inherited from Hegel. Our task is to discover Kierkegaard's politics in the negative critique through which he seeks to rescue dialectical individualism, to repeat, from a Hegelian philosophy that he views as insufficiently faithful to it and from a society of which Hegel's philosophy is an all too faithful expression.

* * * * *

Every individual ought to live in fear and trembling, and so too there is no established order which can do without fear and trembling. Fear and trembling signifies that one is in a process of becoming, and every individual man, and the race as well, is or should be conscious of being in process of becoming. And fear and trembling signifies that a God exists—a fact which no man and no established order dare for an instant forget.[9]

This is Kierkegaard's politics in a nutshell. The fatal flaw of the Hegelian philosophy and of his "present age" is a tendency toward self-deification of the We. *Training in Christianity* carries on a sustained polemic against the deification of the age, the race, the universal, the totality, and the established order, describing it as "the constant rebellion, the permanent revolt against

---

[8]Ibid., 19.

[9]*TC*, 89.

God."[10] The Hegelian philosophy and "the present age" are indicted as co-conspirators in this metaphysical coup d'état.

Kierkegaard develops this politics not only in his late works of social criticism such as *The Attack upon Christendom* but in his first book, *The Concept of Irony*, and throughout his pseudonymous authorship. I want to look especially at *The Concluding Unscientific Postscript*, considered by many to be his most comprehensive and characteristic work. Though it is a major source of support for the standard interpretation of Kierkegaard as a God-and-the-soul-nothing-more philosopher, I believe it offers abundant evidence for the different reading I am suggesting. My clue to reading the *Postscript* is a statement from *The Concept of Irony:* "Irony is a healthiness insofar as it rescues the soul from the snares of relativity."[11] To paraphrase, negative thinking is useful when used to avoid idolatry and absolutizing the merely relative.

In the *Postscript*, Kierkegaard wages war in the name of subjectivity on the world-historically oriented philosophy of Hegel and the world-historically self-contented present age. He seeks to reflect the individual out of the universal, to entice each self to accept the strenuous task of existing as an individual, confronting God and death in time. Such a task must be faced by the individual alone. Social bonds and memberships are useless here. God has no grandchildren, which is to say that we are not saved, in this life or in the life to come, by proper socialization.

Taking subjectivity seriously in this sense means that one

> does not enjoy life in the customary positive and comfortable manner. Most people at a certain point in their search for truth, change. They marry, and they take on a certain position, in consequence of which they feel that they must in all honor have something finished . . . and so they come to think of themselves as really finished. . . . What an affront to God. . . . Living in this manner, one is relieved of the necessity of becoming executively aware of the strenuous difficulties which the simplest of propositions about existing *qua* human-being involves; while on the other hand, as positive thinker, one knows all about world-history, and is fully initiated into the secrets of providence.[12]

What should be noted about this passage is that *Kierkegaard seeks to unsocialize the individual in order to un-deify society.*

Kierkegaard seeks to discomfort those who confuse socialization with salvation; they find their existential task completed when the initiation rites prescribed for adulthood by their society have been completed. Three such rites are mentioned here: marriage, the beginning of family life, work, the beginning of economic activity, and education, initiation into the wisdom of the tribe. It is interesting that Kierkegaard expressly mentions initiation when

---

[10]Ibid.

[11]*CI*, 113.

[12]*CUP*, 78-79.

speaking of a young man's training in the Hegelian philosophy of world history.

But to assume that one's existential task is completed when the individual is brought into right relation with society, that is, when the individual has been socialized, is to absolutize society and confuse society with God. Hence, "What an affront to God." This is why in the *Postscript,* and throughout the authorship, Socrates continually emerges as a hero. He understood, lived, and died the truth that to be a good Athenian one must be more than a good Athenian. In viewing the task of life as greater than assimilating the wisdom and virtue of Athens and its best citizens, Socrates declared allegiance to a god greater than Athens. And in judging him guilty, not of treason but of sacrilege, Athens insisted that it knew no greater god than itself. Socrates' radical individualism, his refusal to identify true virtue with effective socialization, was not his absolutizing of himself as an individual, but his refusal to absolutize Athens. Well aware of his own finitude, expressed in his famous teaching of Socratic ignorance, he was equally aware of the finitude of his society. He knew that both the individual and society must stand in fear and trembling before God. It is easy to understand why Kierkegaard loved him.[13]

The case of Socrates is especially pertinent to our theme because his refusal to absolutize Athens was certainly not the expression of an unpolitical desire to be free from social participation nor an unloyal desire to place his own interests above those of his people. He was as political an animal as has ever lived, and he was so loyal to the laws of Athens, which he viewed as his parents, that he chose rather to die than to repudiate them by escaping.

Kierkegaard makes the same point in another way. One of his earliest complaints against Hegel and his followers is that "the System presupposes faith as something given."[14] He cannot resist the opportunity to tweak Hegel's nose by adding—"and this in a system that is supposed to be without presuppositions!" But this is only a barb. The crucial point is the system's assertion that faith is an immediacy, that philosophy need not concern itself with being edifying, as if faith needed to be engendered or built up, since natural consciousness is religious consciousness. Or to express it differently, since the prephilosophic self is already religious it needs to be led not *to* faith but *from* faith to the more adequate knowledge of God that philosophy offers.

In *Fear and Trembling* the story of Abraham is framed between a preface and epilogue that satirize this notion of going beyond faith, as if it were not

---

[13]By contrast, Hegel develops a sharp critique of personal conscience, both in chapter 6 of the *Phenomenology* and in paragraphs 129-41 of the *Philosophy of Right,* especially paragraph 140. In the former text (Miller translation, 214) he writes, "The wisest men of antiquity have therefore declared that wisdom and virtue consist in living in accordance with the customs of one's nation." And in paragraph 153 of the latter text he favorably quotes a Pythagorean's advice on the ethical education of one's son— "Make him a citizen of a state with good laws."

[14]*CUP,* 18.

the task of a lifetime, as if the man on the street could be assumed to have mastered the acts of faith exemplified by Abraham, father of the faithful.

In the *Postscript,* too, Kierkegaard turns to satire. Suppose, he asks, someone were to be concerned with whether he truly had the right to call himself a Christian.

> He would be smothered in angry glances, and people would say: "How tiresome to make such a fuss about nothing at all; why can't he behave like the rest of us, who are all Christians? It is just as it is with F. F., who refuses to wear a hat on his head like others, but insists on dressing differently." And if he happened to be married, his wife would say to him: "Dear husband of mine, how can you get such notions into your head? How can you doubt that you are a Christian? Are you not a Dane, and does not the geography say that the Lutheran form of the Christian religion is the ruling religion in Denmark? For you are surely not a Jew, nor are you a Mohammedan; what then can you be if not a Christian? It is a thousand years since paganism was driven out of Denmark, so I know you are not a pagan. Do you not perform your duties at the office like a conscientious civil servant; are you not a good citizen of a Christian nation, a Lutheran Christian state? So then of course you must be a Christian."[15]

This particular wife must occasionally pause for breath. When she does, Kierkegaard (through Johannes Climacus) adds this comment: "We have become so objective, it seems, that even the wife of a civil servant argues to the particular individual from the totality, from the state, from the community-idea, from the scientific standpoint of geography."[16]

Notice several things:

1. By arguing from the totality to the particular individual the wife remembers that the I is We but forgets that the We is I. She apparently misunderstands the dialectical nature of spirit as Hegel expounds it in the *Phenomenology.*

2. Hegel, by presupposing faith as given, makes the same mistake. His speculation shows itself at this point to be both (a) a reflection of popular attitudes quite innocent of all philosophy, and (b) thereby a betrayal of his own central philosophical concept.

3. Kierkegaard calls all of this, whether philosophical or popular, objectivity. It is against this kind of thinking that his theory of radical subjectivity is directed. Again we see that his purpose is not to deify the individual but to un-deify society.

4. The tendency of society to deify itself shows up this time in a more subtle form than before. Once again salvation is identified with socialization. By calling itself "a Christian nation," society seems to be placing itself in the role of mediator between God and the individual; but when it simultaneously tells the civil servant that he is simply foolish to worry about his God

---

[15]Ibid., 49.

[16]Ibid., 50.

relationship as long as he is properly related to it, society says in effect, "He who has seen me has seen the Father" and "Whosoever believeth in me hath everlasting life."[17]

Whoever says such things must be divine or blasphemous. Christianity, which teaches that "there is one mediator between God and men, the man Christ Jesus who gave himself as ransom for all," is bound to be offended.[18] Kierkegaard is explicit in rejecting society's claim to be the Son of God. "Man is not related to the ideal through the medium of successive generations, through the State, through the centuries. . . . By reason of the infiltration of the State and social groups and the congregation and society, God can no longer get a hold on the individual. . . . In this way, by the use of the most obliging and courteous philosophic terminology, they have shown Him the door. They are busy about getting a truer and truer conception of God but seem to forget the very first step, that one should fear God. A man who in the objective mass of men is objectively religious does not fear God."[19]

In one respect I am saying nothing new. It has always been clear, I believe, that the issue between Hegel's philosophy and Kierkegaard's faith is that of *apotheosis vs. incarnation. Does the human race become God or does God become human?* I will mention three examples, familiar to readers of the *Postscript,* where the issue is obvious. First, in the famous assertion that a logical system is possible but an existential system impossible, Kierkegaard avoids the affirmation of radical pluralism. "Reality itself is a system," he writes, "for God; but it cannot be a system for any existing spirit."[20] Thus the claim of the Hegelian system to have achieved systematic finality is a thinly disguised attempt to claim divine status for this particular expression of human wisdom.

Second, we see the same thing occurring in the world-historical orientation of the system. For Hegel, borrowing a line from Schiller, *die Weltgeschichte ist das Weltgericht.* Kierkegaard replies, "For God it may perhaps be so. . . . But the human spirit cannot see the world-historical in this manner. . . . World-history is the royal stage where God is spectator, where He is not accidentally but essentially the only spectator, because He is the only one who can be. To this theater no existing spirit has access."[21]

Finally, the identity of thought and being, so basic to Hegelian speculation, evokes the same response. "As soon as the being which corresponds to the truth comes to be empirically concrete, the truth is put in process of becoming, and is again by way of anticipation the conformity of thought with being.

---

[17]John 14:9 and 3:16.

[18]1 Timothy 2:5.

[19]*CUP*, 483-84.

[20]Ibid., 107.

[21]Ibid., 126, 141.

This conformity is actually realized for God, but it is not realized for any existing spirit, who is himself existentially in process of becoming."[22]

These complaints of Kierkegaard have hardly gone unnoticed. However, their political significance is usually overlooked. If we juxtapose them to Kierkegaard's analysis of the young man for whom marriage and his first job are the resolution of all ultimate concerns and of the civil servant who is intimidated into repressing any anxiety about his God relation, we can see that the apotheosis-incarnation issue is not a remote or recondite piece of pure theory. Genuine speculation never is. The question concerns the texture of daily life. Does the individual live with the assurance, conscious (the intellectual person) or unconscious (the common person), that We are absolute—or with the challenge of being, both as I and as We, finite and human before (or possibly without) God?

Hegel is very clear that the speculative apotheosis against which Kierkegaard protests so bitterly is not a personal achievement, but a social and historical one. It is not that Hegel as an isolated individual has achieved divine status; rather he is the verbal expression of the spirit of his age, as Plato and Aristotle were for theirs. It is only because the world spirit has arrived at its present place that his philosophical system is possible. As Hegel says in the preface to the *Philosophy of Right,* "Whatever happens, every individual is a child of his time; so philosophy too is its own time comprehended in thoughts." Thus speculative apotheosis has practical consequences for the world outside of philosophy; but it also stands as the ideological mirror of that world's collective self-image. To a society that inarticulately and thoughtlessly takes itself to be divine, Hegel says, Yes, we are indeed divine, and philosophy can show how this is both possible and necessary.

Kierkegaard wants to preserve the possibility of the Incarnation against this apotheosis of the present age. To do so he insists that the primary We that each of us is is the We constituted by our personal relation to God. In this We, we each remain an I that is responsible for the use of our finite freedom. Exactly the same must be said about the individual as a member of any secondary, human We *and* about each such human We. No family or friendship, no state or society can justly free itself from fear and trembling before God, claiming the individual's absolute allegiance and bestowing upon him or her a share in the divine.

This is clearly a social theory of the human self as the I that is We and the We that is I. But it could easily be argued that it is not in any sense a politics. The argument would be that Kierkegaard sees the tendency toward self-deification by his own society and prophetically speaks out in vehement protest; but this is only a matter of religious interest and not of any intrinsic political significance.

---

[22]Ibid., 170.

There are at least two considerations against this conclusion. In the first place, Kierkegaard sees the ground of mass society and the herd mentality in this tendency of society to deify itself that we have been tracing. He puts it this way:

> The more the collective idea comes to dominate even the ordinary conscious-ness, the more forbidding seems the transition to becoming a particular existing human being instead of losing oneself in the race, and saying "we," "our age," "the nineteenth century." . . . For what does a mere individual count for? Our age knows only too well how little it is, but here also lies the specific immorality of the age. Each age has its own characteristic depravity. Ours is perhaps not plea-sure or indulgence or sensuality, but rather a dissolute pantheistic contempt for the individual man. . . . In the midst of the self-importance of the contemporary generation there is revealed a sense of despair over being human. Everything must attach itself so as to be a part of some movement; men are determined to lose themselves in the totality of things, in world-history, fascinated and deceived by a magic witchery; no one wants to be an individual human being. . . . It cannot be denied that when a man lacks ethical and religious enthusiasm, being a mere individual is a matter for despair—but not otherwise. . . . Just as desert travellers combine into great caravans from fear of robbers and wild beasts, so the individ-uals of the contemporary generation are fearful of existence, because it is god-forsaken; only in great masses do they dare to live, and they cluster together *en masse* in order to feel that they amount to something.[23]

Surely it cannot be said that the phenomena of mass society and herd men-tality are not of fundamental political significance. Any social theory that seeks to understand bureaucracy, prejudice, public opinion, totalitarianism, and the social impact of the media, both as propaganda and as advertising (if there is any difference between the two), will have to comprehend these phenom-ena. The same is true for any social praxis that takes seriously such ideals as community, communication, participation, self-determination, and self-gov-ernment.

But there is a second and even more ominous political consequence of so-cial self-deification. If the "characteristic depravity" or "specific immorality" of the age is that "despair over being human" that generates the herd, this evil is compounded by the fact that the herd is itself amoral. Kierkegaard's regular lament in the *Postscript* is that "the system has no ethics." This seems like an unfair criticism of Hegel, since it is the ethical task of the individual to tran-scend particularity and conform to the universal, to exhibit as a matter of character and behavior the values expressed in the laws and customs of his or her people. The problem is that the universal, which is not an abstract,

---

[23]Ibid., 317-18. The pantheism Kierkegaard speaks of is the same as the "collective idea" he refers to at the beginning of the passage. We could call it social pantheism. This political theology is an attempt to avoid the godforsakenness of those who know no other god. For Kierkegaard, as for Nietzsche, after we kill God we make ourselves into God.

metaphysical entity, but a concrete historical people, nation, or state, is itself without moral obligations as soon as it has been absolutized. As divine, its will is law and all its deeds are good.

Loosing this human God upon the earth is clearly a matter of political import. Technologically its power is virtually unlimited, and morally its power is actually unchecked. It is here, Kierkegaard suspects, that the maxim of Lord Acton will be fulfilled, that absolute power corrupts absolutely.[24] Thus his manifesto begins with the words, there is a specter haunting the world. Its name is neither communism nor capitalism, but something capable of existing in either form. It is the amoral herd. It expresses the ultimate irony, that when human society insists on being something more than human, it ends up as something catastrophically less than human. How prophetically did Hobbes speak when he called this Leviathan an "artificial animal." For while it is indeed a human product, it is a beast and not something human. Just as the debate between communism and capitalism can never be fundamental from the perspective of Kierkegaard's politics, so the debate between materialism and idealism will always remain penultimate. The simple mention of "Leviathan" makes it clear that the amoral herd can find its ideological justification in Hobbes as easily as in Hegel. The truly basic question remains whether we can or cannot become God.

* * * * *

Kierkegaard's politics has had an interesting career in the existentialist tradition. Few, if any, outside that tradition have offered such a penetrating analysis of the herd and its uncommitted anonymity as Nietzsche and Heidegger, Ortega and Marcel. Each has reiterated and refined Kierkegaard's claim that the fundamental political question is not the shape of society's institutions but the quality of its spirit. Character is more basic than constitution.[25]

The most striking reaffirmation of Kierkegaard's politics, however, is that of Camus in *The Rebel*. It is striking not only in its vivid account of the terror that self-deified humanity unleashes upon itself, but also in the profound agreement between militant unbeliever and militant believer in identifying the "characteristic depravity" or "specific immorality" of the age. Camus' story illustrates "legalized murder" from 1789 to 1848 to 1917 and eventually to Mussolini, Hitler, and Stalin. Representing the inner side of the outward terror and bloodshed, Camus sees not simply a morality of justifying means by reference to ends, but a moral nihilism that rejects all limits and replaces ques-

---

[24]Power also corrupts individuals. But Napoleon had his Waterloo and Nixon his Watergate. Idi Amin and the Shah of Iran cannot survive indefinitely. Meanwhile, the amoral herd long survives the coming and going of individual leaders.

[25]This is not to affirm the primacy of private over public morality, as if personal morality were independent of social structures. It is rather to say that society has an inward and an outward dimension and the former is basic. As a society thinks in its heart, so shall it be.

tions of right and good with questions of power and efficiency. The major premise for the moral nihilism that produces political cynicism is theological, the death of God *and* the logically inconsequent but historically actual deification of human society. As sacred and absolute, "the people" are constrained by no law but are themselves the sovereign of history. Their self-appointed representatives have a kind of cosmic, executive privilege that inevitably produces the kinds of cosmic Watergates we've seen from Robespierre to Auschwitz.

Thus the basic story is the "history of European pride," the metaphysical rebellion underlying historical atrocities. Ivan Karamazov and Friedrich Nietzsche tell this story best. Because of the suffering of innocent children, Ivan feels compelled to deny God and truth. He concludes that "everything is permitted" and ends up, almost against his will, taking himself seriously and permitting murder. Nietzsche, too, affirms the death of God. He doesn't exactly intend it, but his Yea-saying, his *amor fati,* his total acceptance leave him no ground to refuse murder and once again everything is permitted. Nietzsche makes this conclusion almost inescapable by explicitly assigning humans the task of becoming God to take the place of the God who died.

Ivan and Nietzsche may have said it most succinctly, but they did not say it first. Camus traces the theory of human apotheosis back through Marx and Hegel to Rousseau as well as through its literary ancestry.

I suggested earlier that Kierkegaard's politics has considerable contemporary significance. Camus allows us to see this more clearly. His story is not just about a past in which thinkers killed God and politicians killed God's children. It is a story about our present, which he did not live to see. In discussing the crimes of communist and fascist totalitarianism he notes the partnership of ideology and technology, the one removing moral limits, the other removing practical limits to power. He also notes that the old ideological state has usually been replaced by the new industrial state, that economics has increasingly triumphed over political ideology in the strictest sense. This could be reassuring, but it is not. The new industrial state has its own ideology. Camus calls it the "myth of unlimited production." This myth shares with the earlier ideologies the replacement of moral with technological questions. Means become ends and anything feasible is permissible. Efficacy replaces ethics. So nothing has really changed, since this has increasingly been the premise of our history for the past several centuries.[26] Camus is sure that "the myth of unlimited production brings war in its train as inevitably as clouds announce a storm."[27] The replacement of the fanatical ideologue with the suave manager is only a cosmetic change.

------

[26]For a provocative development of this theme, see Jürgen Habermas, "The Classical Doctrine of Politics in Relation to Social Philosophy," in *Theory and Practice,* trans. John Viertel (Boston: Beacon Press, 1973).

[27]Albert Camus, *The Rebel,* trans. Anthony Bower (New York: Alfred A. Knopf, 1956) 275.

Camus pleads for a politics that will acknowledge limits. He even says that politics "must submit to the eternal verities."[28] Camus concludes on a note of hope for his brothers and sisters. They may learn to live again instead of kill, "but on condition that it is understood that they correct one another, and that a limit, under the sun, shall curb them all. *Each tells the other that he is not God.*"[29] It is not clear whether each says "I am not God" or "You are not God." Kierkegaard does not quibble. Camus is a pagan, like Lessing and Socrates, with whom Kierkegaard proudly associates.

---

[28]Ibid., 298.

[29]Ibid., 306. My italics.

chapter

Kierkegaard's Sociology

4

Hegel describes philosophy as "its own time comprehended in thought."[1] In spite of their many problems with Hegel, Kierkegaard and his spiritual contemporary, Nietzsche, agree on this definition. But whereas Hegel meant to penetrate the world-historical significance of the French Revolution,[2] Kierkegaard and Nietzsche do not primarily direct their attention to such events as the revolutions of 1848 or the unification of Germany and the Franco-Prussian war. Instead they see their task as interpreting a sociological event, the emergence of mass society, the crowd, the public, the herd. They agree in viewing their own time as engaged in a life-or-death struggle with this debilitating disease and (against Marx) in viewing the phenomena of mass society as epiphenomena of a spiritual condition rather than of economic structures.[3] Thus this sociological event is intimately related to a parallel, "religious" event, the death of God, or, in Kierkegaard's language, the disappearance of Christianity from Christendom. The massification of society is the flip side of its secularization.

Still, this agreement is anything but complete. From Nietzsche's perspective, the herd is born of a passion for leveling, which has its own origin in a resentment and envy that religion masks as the ideals of justice and equality. This "Christian" morality is all that remains of a religious heritage that the modern world has, for the most part, disowned. The "herd" is Nietzsche's name for the disease that occurs when people only incompletely break free from Christianity, retaining its morality while repudiating its metaphysics.

---

[1]From the preface to the *Philosophy of Right*.

[2]See Joachim Ritter, "Hegel and the French Revolution," in *Hegel and the French Revolution: Essays on the Philosophy of Right,* Richard Dien Winfield, trans. (Cambridge: MIT Press, 1982) and Jürgen Habermas, "Hegel's Critique of the French Revolution," in *Theory and Practice,* John Viertel, trans. (Boston: Beacon Press, 1973).

[3]Implicit here is the suggestion that Marx and Weber have not exhausted the possibilities for a sociology of capitalist society.

Health can be achieved only by making this break wholehearted and complete.

Kierkegaard's diagnosis and prescription is equally "spiritual" but quite the converse. The herd—this is a term he also uses to talk about mass society—is the offspring of a passionless age, committed only to self-interest. The envy that generates leveling betrays the increasingly total absence of ideals from social life, though a lot of talk about God remains. The profession of "Christian" metaphysics is all that remains of a religious heritage that the modern world has eviscerated. The herd is Kierkegaard's name for the disease that occurs when people only incompletely adhere to Christianity, retaining its metaphysics while repudiating its morality.[4] Health can be achieved only by a wholehearted and complete return to true faith.[5]

It is his account of mass society that is referred to when speaking of Kierkegaard's sociology, and this essay describes that sociology. It is not only of interest because of its suggested link with the works of Hegel, Marx, and Nietzsche; beyond that is its immediate bearing on our own times. Kierkegaard offers us a shoe that fits embarrassingly well. At times it appears that he knows us better than we know ourselves.

Though Kierkegaard's sociology is found throughout his writings, this essay focuses primarily on a rather lengthy book review that Kierkegaard published under the title *Two Ages—The Age of Revolution and the Present Age: A Literary Review*, along with materials from the journals on themes central to the review. This little book has had a remarkable, though to my knowledge untraced, history within the existentialist tradition, and the portion of it that most directly sets forth Kierkegaard's sociology has been available to the English-speaking world since 1940 under the title *The Present Age*.[6]

The novel that Kierkegaard reviews is itself entitled *Two Ages*. His summary of its plot suggests that the soap opera was invented in Denmark, but he keeps insisting that it is a work of genuine literary merit. His primary concern, however, is not literary. Kierkegaard sees the lives and loves of the numerous characters mirroring the essential features of two distinct cultures,

---

[4]See *TA*, 77 and 81. Feuerbach makes a similar observation, describing a modern "believer" as follows: "He denies God practically by his conduct—the world has possession of all his thoughts and inclinations—but he does not deny him theoretically, he does not attack his existence; he lets that rest. But his existence does not affect or incommode him." *The Essence of Christianity*, George Eliot, trans. (New York: Harper and Brothers, 1957) 15.

[5]This theme of the necessity of true religion runs throughout *TA;* see 81-82, 87-88, and 108.

[6]The full title is *The Present Age and Two Minor Ethico-Religious Treatises*, Alexander Dru, trans. (Oxford: Oxford University Press, 1940). In 1962 Harper & Row replaced one of the "minor" treatises with an introduction by Walter Kaufman and republished it under the title *The Present Age*.

the age of the French Revolution and the present age. (The novel was published in 1845, the review in 1846, about a month after *The Concluding Unscientific Postscript* appeared.)

Perhaps it seemed providential to Kierkegaard to come across this novel
while completing the writing of the *Postscript;* for its characters (at least as
he sees them) embody his own distinction between subjectivity and objectivity and permit him to restate that distinction as the opposition of passion and
reflection. When he says repeatedly that the revolutionary age was an age of
passion, while the present age is one of reflection, his point is to describe and
evaluate the present age from the perspective of the ethicoreligious subjectivity developed in his pseudonymous authorship, which culminated in the
Postscript.

This is not to say that the revolutionary age was a paradigm of the ethicoreligious subjectivity Kierkegaard sought to evoke. It was not. He cannot, for
example, approve of the revolutionary age's disrespect for marriage nor of the
affairs that occur outside of its bonds in the first part of the novel. Even so,
he sees an essential passion at work, which "is its own guarantee that there
is something sacred. . . . But prosiness lacks the concept. Thus when a revolutionary age tolerates a relation to a married woman, it has an idea of propriety despite its false concept . . . [the] propriety that it be concealed."[7] In
the middle of this passage Kierkegaard explicitly evokes a crucial passage from
the *Postscript*:

> If one who lives in the midst of Christendom goes up to the house of God, the
> house of the true God, with the true conception of God in his knowledge, and
> prays, but prays in a false spirit; and one who lives in an idolatrous community
> prays with the entire passion of the infinite, although his eyes rest upon the image
> of an idol: where is there most truth? The one prays in truth to God though he
> worships an idol; the other prays falsely to the true God, and hence worships in
> fact an idol.[8]

Kierkegaard praises neither adultery nor idolatry. He raises a question of inwardness, whether outwardly "proper" behavior and "correct" beliefs without the passionate commitment appropriate to them are worth much.

Kierkegaard's praise of passion is not a carte blanche invitation to anything
that presents itself as an urge. "Let no one interpret all my talk about pathos
[*Pathos*] and passion [*Liedenskab*] to mean that I intend to sanction every
uncircumcised immediacy, every unshaven passion."[9] What then is the "essential passion," the "passion of the infinite" that he admires in the revolutionary age in spite of its adultery and in the pagan in spite of his idolatry?
Kierkegaard has already told us. It is the passion that grows out of the con-

---

[7]*TA,* 64.

[8]*CUP,* 179-80.

[9]*JP,* 3:3127.

viction "that there is something sacred." The sacred may be misidentified as earthly eros, the "provisional idea" mistaken for the "highest idea." Still, this is better than the "prosiness [that] lacks the concept" and the "fossilized formalism" that preside over human sexuality when nothing at all is still sacred. The pagan may have a false concept of God, but at least "he has the idea that one should fear God."[10]

Here Kierkegaard links the notions of "the sacred" and "the idea." He uses the latter expression most frequently. This is the clue to a distinction between passion and reflection. An initial indication of what he means by the idea can be found by recalling a frequently quoted passage from the Gilleleie journal of 1835. "The crucial thing is to find a truth which is truth *for me*, to find *the idea for which I am willing to live and die* . . . of what use would it be to me for truth to stand before me, cold and naked, not caring whether or not I acknowledged it. . . . What is truth but to live for an idea?"[11] The animal lives out of instinct; we, as spirit, can live for an idea. The animal dies out of necessity; we, as spirit, can give our life because there is something worth dying for. To live, not out of habit but because one knows why life is worth living, and to die, not out of necessity, but because one values something more than life itself—that is to be related to the idea. The idea is a truth that claims me for its own in life and in death and, in claiming me, gives meaning to both life and death.[12]

Passion, then, is the driving force of a life lived in touch with this idea. Reflection is thought's ability to talk its way out of this relation.[13]

But why would thought want to talk its way free of the idea? We are not talking, of course, about thought in general, for thought is always someone's thought, and the question should more properly be phrased: Why would anyone want to talk his or her way free of the idea? The answer is quite simple if one pays attention to the way in which Kierkegaard uses the term *idea*. It is virtually interchangeable with the term *ideal*, and he views it as providing life's norm, demand, criterion, and requirement. As if to undercut the subtle distinctions of our own moral philosophy, he sees the idea as the individual's

---

[10]*TA*, 64-65. The distinction between the provisional and highest ideas is a clear reference to the theory of love and beauty in Plato's *Symposium*.

[11]*JP*, 5:5100.

[12]A classical Christian expression of this idea is the opening of the *Heidelberg Catechism:* "What is your only comfort, in life and in death? That I belong—body and soul, in life and in death—not to myself but to my faithful Savior, Jesus Christ."

[13]Reflection, as the thoughtful complement to sheer immediacy and enthusiasm, has its proper place (*TA*, 96, 110-11). It can even be used to help free the self of reflection in the sense described here (*JP*, 3:3129). Kierkegaard's complaint is not against reflection as such, but against reflection cut off from passion. This reflection lacks not only the commitment that passion involves, but serves as a defense against both commitment and passion.

telos *and* duty. And he frequently qualifies these normative terms that contextually define "the idea" with the term *infinite* to make it clear that the idea makes unconditional and ultimate demands of our existence. The idea wounds and makes life strenuous; its absence makes life easier. It does not merely demand that I abandon my criminal or immoral ways and conform to the prevailing mores of my society; it subjects social morality itself to the test of an infinite demand and deprives social conformity of an ultimate comfort. The idea tells me, as it told Socrates of old, that to be a good Athenian one must be more than a good Athenian.[14] So there's not really much mystery about why thought might choose to loosen its links with the idea.

But what has all this to do with Kierkegaard's sociology? The themes of passion, reflection, and the idea provide an elegant restatement of the subjectivity and inwardness motifs of the *Postscript,* and we have just seen that the idea makes *every* social morality and socialization process relative.[15] But the very inclusiveness of that "every" raises a question whether all this has any particular bearing on the phenomena of mass society, a distinctively modern kind of social formation.

Kierkegaard views the individual and society as standing in a relation of dialectical interaction. Though neither unilaterally conditions the other, they are mutually determined by each other. There is thus an important isomorphism between them, the one reflecting the character of the other; and the primacy of passion or reflection in the individuals who make up society will be an index of that society's shape. Mass society is the society that is produced by, and in turn produces, individuals in which reflection predominates and the idea is essentially absent. (Other societies distinguish themselves by different versions of the idea that underlie their passions.)

Thus the categories we have explored are the keys to Kierkegaard's sociology, which he summarizes as follows:

> Purely dialectically the relations are as follows, and let us think them through dialectically without considering any specific age. When individuals (each one individually) are essentially and passionately related to an idea and together are essentially related to the same idea, the relation is optimal and normative. Individually the relation separates them (each one has himself for himself), and ideally it unites them. . . . Thus the individuals never come too close to each other in the herd sense, simply because they are united on the basis of an ideal distance.[16]

---

[14]*JP*, 2:1770-1825. Also see above, "Kierkegaard's Politics," 35.

[15]This strikes at the heart of Hegel's agreement with Aristotle on the link between politics and ethics.

[16]*TA*, 62-63.

It is important to notice that Kierkegaard distinguishes two ways of deviat-
ing from this norm.[17] They invite the labels "barbarism" and "decadence."

> [I]f individuals relate to an idea merely *en masse* (consequently without the in-
> dividual separation of inwardness), we get violence, anarchy, riotousness; but if
> there is no idea for the individuals *en masse* and no individually separating es-
> sential inwardness, either, then we have crudeness. . . . Remove the relation to
> oneself, and we have the tumultuous self-relating of the mass to an idea; but re-
> move this as well, and we have crudeness.[18]

A decadent society will inevitably think itself superior to a barbaric society,
for it enjoys an orderliness that contrasts sharply with the latter's tumultuous
anarchy and riotous violence. Ever the Socratic gadfly, Kierkegaard challenges the self-evidence of this superiority. After all, he insists, the barbaric
society has at least retained a partial relation to the idea, while the decadent
society, beneath its facade of civilization, has lost contact with the idea both
individually and collectively. To render the issue concrete and contemporary,
Kierkegaard asks the infuriating but carefully grounded question whether civilized Western societies such as our own are perhaps further from being truly
civilized than Cambodia under the Khmer Rouge or Iran under the Ayatollah
Khomeini.

In any case it is clear when Kierkegaard speaks of the herd that typifies the
modern age that it is the decadent society—or in his words, the crude society—that he has in mind. Because of its double loss of contact with the idea,
he views it as 1) a subhuman society, 2) an amoral society, 3) a diabolical
society, and 4) a society of glittering vices.

* * * * *

1. The very use of the term *herd* to describe mass society implies sinking from
a genuinely human level of existence to a merely animal level. For Kierkegaard the term *sinking* is especially appropriate, while the term *merely* is not
quite right. We are by nature both animal and spirit. We are not discussing
an evolutionary situation in which we have not yet risen or emerged from our
animal nature to a truly human nature. Thus to become a herd is to sink, to
fall below what one already is. But since we are spirit by nature we cannot
become simply or merely animal, and the human herd will always be distinctively human. It presupposes, for example, envy, which the animal herd
lacks.

> "Just like the others." This phrase expresses the two characteristic marks of
> being man in general: (1) sociality, the animal-creature which is linked to the herd:
> just like the others; (2) envy, which however, animals do not have.

---

[17]In reply to a question about the establishment of this norm, Kierkegaard might
well respond in the manner of Hegel in the *Philosophy of History*, that it has already
been established, so far as it can be in the pseudonymous writings, *and* that it will
establish itself in use throughout the the critical descriptions that follow.

[18]*TA*, 63.

This envy is very characteristic. To be specific, animals are not envious because each animal is only a copy or specimen [*Exemplar*]. Man, on the other hand, is the only animal species in which every specimen . . . is an individuality, intended [*lagt an*] to be spirit. Number or the numerical man, of course, does not become spirit but still retains this feature which distinguishes him from other animal creatures—envy.[19]

This envy that insists that everyone be just like the others is essential to the leveling process by which the herd is born. It presents itself under the honorific label of equality, but Kierkegaard sees it as a form of escapism. In a revolutionary age talk of equality may well have represented a passion to provide full human dignity to those who had previously been denied it by systems of political and economic domination; but in the present age it softens the spiritual requirements that are an essential ingredient in human dignity. Thus the slogans of equality serve not so much to elevate individuals to the dignity of being human as to free them from the responsibility of rising to this vocation.

This escapism is in the direction of a purely animal existence. "The animal's notion of being safe when it is in the flock, that danger consists in being separated from the flock," is all the animal knows, for "*the animal creature needs no higher certainty than numbers.*" Since "man is *by nature* an animal-creation," it follows that "[a]ll human effort is therefore in the direction of running together in a herd." But it is not that simple. We are also spirit and as such we feel "the need for a kind of certainty other than numbers," other than being just like all the others. "Yet the natural man, the animal-man, shrinks from becoming [spirit]," and the reason is clear. "The truth is that in the herd one is free from the criterion of the individual and of the ideal."[20] Mass society is a flight from spirit. It is a state in which those who are a polar tension of nature and spirit play the role of the animals they can never be. It is the shared bad faith by which individuals help each other sustain the illusion that they can shirk their spiritual destiny by joining the public.[21] But "the crowd is untruth" just because it is this choice to free itself from the idea.[22]

2. It becomes clearer that the herd is an amoral society. The idea from which it seeks to free itself by huddling together is the ideal, a source of that unconditional claim upon human existence that constitutes moral life. This is not to say that the herd has no values; rather, a transvaluation of values has occurred in which moral values have been replaced by other values. The categories of moral life are taken out of play and no longer function as the conditions of possible experience.

---

[19]*JP*, 3:2986. Cf. *TA*, 81-84.

[20]*JP*, 3:298, 2970, 2980.

[21]The theme of self-deception emerges in *TA* at 8, 10, and 77.

[22]This phrase is the constant refrain of the first of the two notes on "the individual," written in 1846 and published in *PV*.

The revolutionary age is a passionate age, that is, one related to the idea. This means "it has *not nullified the principle of contradiction* and can become either good or evil." It lives in a framework for which the distinction between good and evil, right and wrong, is essential to decision and action. The herd is a society that, by freeing itself from the idea, has freed itself from this opposition or contradiction as well. But this means that from the moral point of view neither the herd nor the individuals who belong to it can be said to choose or act. Instead they remain, like King Agrippa, in "the most enervating state imaginable."[23]

In his pseudonymous writings Kierkegaard calls this choice not to choose, this freely adopted amorality, the aesthetic stage of existence. Those earlier discussions are brought to mind by a second way in which Kierkegaard refers to the amorality of mass society. Three times on a single page he tells us that "the public is unrepentant."[24] In a related passage he writes that "a crowd in its very concept is the untruth, by reason of the fact that it renders the individual completely impenitent and irresponsible, or at least weakens his sense of responsibility by reducing it to a fraction."[25] The amorality of this world in which neither responsibility nor repentance have a place can also be expressed by saying, "The sum and substance of the public life is actually, from first to last, lack of conscience."[26]

What especially links this portrayal of mass society to the pseudonymous description of the aesthetic stage is the account of what replaces moral seriousness. This unrepentant public is "that gallery public [that] now seeks to be entertained and indulges in the notion that everything anyone does is done so that it may have something to gossip about. . . . If I were to imagine this public as a person . . . I most likely would think of one of the Roman emperors, an imposing, well-fed figure suffering from boredom and, therefore, craving only the sensate titillation of laughter. . . . So this person, more sluggish than he is evil . . . saunters around looking for variety." Along with the author of "The Rotation Method," the crowd believes that "boredom is the root of all evil."[27]

For the amoral herd that fears boredom above all else, everything becomes entertainment. Sex and sport, politics and the arts are transformed into en-

---

[23]*TA*, 66.

[24]Ibid., 95.

[25]*PV*, 112. Cf. 116 and *JP*, 3:2932.

[26]*JP*, 3:2955.

[27]*TA*, 94 and *EO*, 1:281. The last two essays of *EO*, vol. 1, "The Rotation Method" and "Diary of a Seducer," give special emphasis to the place of boredom and "the interesting" in the pre-ethical stage of existence. Cf. Gabriel Marcel, "The Mystery of the Family," in *Homo Viator*, Emma Craufurd, trans. (New York: Harper & Row, 1962) 82-84.

tertainment. Even religion will have to become show business if it is to survive. Nothing is immune from the demand that boredom be relieved (but
without personal involvement, for mass society is a spectator society). If television does not yet exist in this society, it will have to be invented.

The link between an entertainment ethos and the media is perhaps more
obvious for us than it was for Kierkegaard. But his discussion of the amorality
of the herd gives special attention to "the press," which he views as essential
to the creation of "the public."[28] Biographically it is clear that the press becomes an issue for him by virtue of the *Corsair* affair rather than his pseudonymous discussion of boredom and "the interesting." Still, he views it as
contributing, by means of its impersonality and anonymity, to the loss of a
sense of responsibility (the central issue).[29] Consequently, "the Jesuits in their
degeneracy were the most disgraceful attempt to seize control of conscien-
ces. The daily press is the most infamous attempt to constitute the lack of
conscience as a principle of the state and of humanity."[30] The media research
that could be generated by taking that last sentence seriously might well be
called Socratic sociology, for, like Kierkegaard, Socrates thought you could
understand a society only by examining its commitment to the good.

Kierkegaard views mass society as leaving the distinction between good and
evil outside its world view. One way this happens is through the replacement
of such notions as responsibility and repentance with talk about "the boring"
and "the interesting." Another way of achieving the same goal emerges in the
third reference of *Two Ages* to the herd's amorality. This is his complaint about
the herd's "habitual and excessive relativity."[31]

Kierkegaard seems to have two things in mind here; a calculative and a
comparative mentality. The calculative tendency is linked with procrastina-
tion, but we should not read this as if nothing ever happened. The calculative
habit focuses on the effectiveness of means in relation to ends, and this makes
it easy to avoid moral questions about both ends and means. In Kantian language, the calculative mentality deals only with hypothetical, and never with
categorical imperatives. In a world where this thinking prevails a great deal
may happen, but none of it is worthy of the name of human action from the
perspective of the ethicoreligious subjectivity that is Kierkegaard's norm.

The comparative tendency brackets basic moral questions by focusing on
another relation, that of my behavior or our behavior to the behavior of others. "Everyone, everyone is so prone to set his mind at ease in a relativity. Anyone who is a little better than his family and relatives or the others in the
provincial town where he lives or among his peers, etc., promptly sets his mind

[28]*TA*, 90-94.

[29]*JP*, 2:2152.

[30]Ibid., 2:2168.

[31]*TA*, 70.

at ease and feels superior." "The law of existence for the numerical or for mass men is that they live by comparisons."[32]

At the time when the president of Yale University publicly raised the question whether a Black Panther could get a fair trial in the American courts, I remember discussing the question with a national religious leader. The reply was the solemn assurance that our system was surely to be preferred to the Soviet system. That the answer came from one who loudly asserts the reality of moral absolutes would not persuade Kierkegaard that he had not been brainwashed by "habitual and excessive relativity, " an earmark of the amoral herd.

3. The diabolical character of mass society is grounded in this amorality. Nietzsche's madman announces, "God is dead. God remains dead. And we have killed him. How shall we comfort ourselves, the murderers of all murderers? . . . Must we ourselves not become gods simply to appear worthy of it?"[33] Nietzsche sees the herd as unable to comfort itself in this way because it remains too tied to the morality of good and evil. By contrast, Kierkegaard sees the very amorality of the herd to be the ground of its own eventually demonic self-deification.[34] The first step can be described as follows: "Therefore mankind felt an unspeakable relief when it got Christianity turned around in such a way that it got rid of God and Christianity came to mean there is no duty toward God. Man thinks he will have the easiest time of all when there is no God at all—then man can play the lord. After that God becomes at most a handsome ornament, a luxury item—for there is no duty toward God."[35]

This religious implication of the herd's amorality can be described as *atheism* ("But from an ethico-religious point of view, to recognize the 'crowd' as the court of last resort is to deny God") or as *pantheism* ("All doubt has ultimately its stronghold in the illusion of temporal existence that we are, a lot of us, pretty much the whole of humanity, which in the end can jolly well overawe God and be itself the Christ. And pantheism is an acoustic illusion which confounds *vox populi* with *vox dei*") or as *idolatry* ("The idol, the tyrant, of our age is 'the many,' 'the crowd,' statistics").[36]

In *Two Ages* the language of idolatry prevails. We have already seen Kierkegaard compare mass society unfavorably with paganism, and now a slightly

---

[32]*JP*, 3:2966, 2986.

[33]See par. 125 of *The Gay Science*. This is translated by Walter Kaufmann, and appears in several editions.

[34]This is a central theme of ch.3, "Kierkegaard's Politics."

[35]*JP*, 2:1808.

[36]*PV*, 118, 135; *JP*, 3:2951. In *JP*, 3:2942, Kierkegaard notes that it is from this *vox populi* that the cry goes up: "Crucify! Crucify!" He calls this pantheism because the divine has become wholly immanent, not in nature but in society. See n. 23 of the previous chapter.

different aspect of that comparison emerges. "When passion is essentially present in the pagan, [essential passion = living before the Idea] even his idolatry is not devoid of devoutness; although he has a false concept, he has the idea that one should fear God."[37] In other words, the pagan idolatry Kierkegaard has in mind falls short of self-deification and preserves an understanding of God as morally transcendent to both the individual and society. The implicit comparison, that the present age has lost even this sense that "one should fear God," is made explicit in the journals. By virtue of becoming the crowd Christendom has become "a far more serious battle against God than man's battle against God in paganism ever was."[38]

It is not surprising that self-deification should be seen as a particularly pernicious form of idolatry. The Christian tradition (with special help from Milton) has identified the serpent of Genesis 3 and the King of Babylon whose fall is described in Isaiah 14 as Satan. The fall of Satan and the human fall represent the entry of evil into the universe and into human history. In both cases the story of origin is also a story of essence, and the secret of sin is exposed as rebellious pride that insists on becoming like God, obliterating the difference between creature and Creator. Since Kierkegaard sees the crowd that is Christendom as practicing this rebellious pride, we might expect him to see the idolatry of the present age as demonic. He does not disappoint us. (Remember in reading the following quotation that reflection here signifies the attempt of thought to free itself from the idea.)

> The idolized positive principle of sociality in our age is the consuming, demoralizing principle that in the thralldom of reflection transforms even virtues into *vitia splendida* [glittering vices]. And what is the basis of this other than a disregard for the separation of the religious individual before God in the responsibility of eternity. When dismay commences at this point, one seeks comfort in company, and thus reflection captures the individual for his whole life. . . . Leveling is not the action of one individual, but a reflection-game in the hand of an abstract power. . . . While the individual egotistically thinks he knows what he is doing, it must be said that they all know not what they do; for just as inspired enthusiastic unanimity results in a something more that is not the individuals', a something more emerges here also. A demon that no individual can control is conjured up.[39]

That the present age is one of reflection is the constant refrain of *Two Ages.* By now there is nothing especially surprising in the triple reference to reflection in this passage so far as it a) moves effortlessly between individual and society (since Kierkegaard views them as dialectically interdependent), b) identifies reflection with a loss of responsibility, and c) views this loss as idolatry. It is important to note the triple reference to reflection as bondage in

---

[37]*TA*, 64.

[38]*JP*, 3:2992.

[39]*TA*, 86.

this chapter. Modern society is "in the thralldom of reflection." "Reflection captures the individual for life." And the leveling process that belongs essentially to the herd is "a reflection-game in the hand of an abstract power" rather than any genuinely human action.

Living in a godless society the individual "seeks comfort in company." This company is "a something more" than the individuals who make it up. But it is not a human We which transcends the human I's who make it up. It is no voluntary association as Locke would have it, nor a moral commonwealth as Rousseau and Kant would have it, nor the incarnate spirit of a nation as Fichte and Hegel would have it. It is an "abstract power," which, though not human, holds human beings in bondage. It is "a demon." Through satanic pride a demonic power has been conjured up, and modern mass society is itself this demonic power.[40]

This network of thoughts may throw some light on a rather puzzling passage in the introduction to *Two Ages*. There Kierkegaard describes the youth who speaks *"in the name of age* concerning the demands of the times" as giving the impression "that an intoxicated divinity is speaking, least of all an individual human being."[41] The image of the intoxicated divinity suggests something from a Dionysiac revel. The following journal entry from 1850 might well be taken as a commentary on press secretaries for the present age as drunken deities.

> In contrast to what was said about possession in the Middle Ages and times like that, that there were individuals who sold themselves to the devil, I have an urge to write a book:
>   Possession and Obsession in Modern Times
> and show how people *en masse* abandon themselves to it, how it is now carried on *en masse*. This is why people run together in flocks—so that natural and animal rage will grip a person, so that he feels stimulated, inflamed, and *ausser sich*. The scenes on Bloksberg are utterly pedantic compared to this demonic lust, a lust to lose oneself in order to evaporate in a potentiation, so that a person is outside of himself, does not really know what he is doing or what he is saying or who it is or what it is speaking through him, while the blood rushes faster, the eyes glitter and stare fixedly, the passions boil, lusts seethe.[42]

Kierkegaard is not complaining here about the sexual revolution. Sex is just a metaphor for people running together in flocks to lose themselves in a distinctively modern kind of possession. Mass society is not only demonic be-

---

[40]See *JP*, 2:2152, 2164-65. Also compare *TA*, 81 where reflection is described as a vast penitentiary. Kierkegaard's sociological analysis of demonic powers relates directly to a number of contemporary discussions of the "principalities and powers" in Pauline theology. See John Howard Yoder, *The Politics of Jesus* (Grand Rapids: Eerdmans, 1972) ch. 8, and for a partial bibliography, n. 4 on 142.

[41]*TA*, 9.

[42]*JP*, 4:4178.

cause of the superhuman (but godless) power it holds over people; it is demonic as the metaphysical *Walpurgisnacht* that enables them to give themselves over to this power and be possessed by it. Just as decent, civilized people are shocked and offended by Goethe's essentially medieval portrayal of demonic revelry, Kierkegaard intends those who are ethicoreligiously serious to be horrified at this picture of the modern world they belong to. He might well have used the words of Marx, "The people must be put in *terror* of themselves in order to give them *courage.*"[43]

What features of the modern world are to be interpreted by these images? We must not think too hastily of German masses whipped into a frenzy by Hitler's rhetoric, nor American youth screaming "Hell no! We won't go!" nor Iranian throngs shaking their fists and chanting against the Shah and Americans. These scenes fit the imagery of Walpurgis night, and Kierkegaard's analysis certainly applies to them; but they are examples of what was previously called the barbaric society, in which individuals relate en masse to the idea in some form, whereas the prime focus of *Two Ages* is on a decadent society that he calls crude—the terribly civilized society in which he and we live.

We need to remember that whatever delight Mephistopheles takes in escorting Faust to the Bloksberg, his normal pose is that of a suave and debonair man of the world. Similarly, in the New Testament the Devil is a "roaring lion, looking for someone to devour," but he is more frequently described as a clever trickster who "disguises himself as an angel of light."[44] We should therefore not be surprised if the forms of possession Kierkegaard invites us to examine have the appearance of civilized respectability rather than Dionysian revelry. This only means, in the light of his analysis, that we have to look harder to perceive the demonic aspect. He calls our attention to a marketing executive intoxicated with market shares, and a TV mogul intoxicated with Nielsen ratings; an economist who has sold his soul to the theory of growth, and a conglomerate chairman who has sold his soul to its practice; a philosopher who defines rationality as the effective calculation of means toward ends, and a scientist who practices this rationality; an educator who confuses ignorance reduction with education, and a religious leader who confuses church growth with evangelism. The passions that underlie all this civilized dedication may be viewed as seething lust just to the degree that reflection has freed them from the service of the idea. It is the best and the brightest who reveal most clearly the demonic nature of the present age.

4. A fourth and final conceptual weapon that Kierkegaard wields against modern mass society is in the notion of virtues as glittering vices. We have already noted the crucial passage. "The idolized positive principle of soci-

---

[43]From "A Contribution to the Critique of Hegel's Philosophy of Right. Introduction," in *Karl Marx: Early Writings*, Rodney Livingstone and Gregor Benton, trans. (New York: Random House, 1975) 247.

[44]1 Peter 5:8 and 2 Cor. 11:14. Cf. Eph. 6:11, 1 Tim. 3:7, 2 Tim. 2:26, and Rev. 20:10.

ality in our age is the consuming, demoralizing principle that in the thralldom of reflection transforms even virtues into *vitia splendida* [glittering vices]." Kierkegaard had already used this idea in the *Philosophical Fragments* and would use it again in *Works of Love*.[45]

Though it originates with the church fathers' (Lactantius's and Augustine's) critique of paganism, it is the point at which Kierkegaard's critique is most Nietzschean. Just as when the virtuous say "I am just" [*Ich bin gerecht*], Nietzsche hears "I am revenged" [*Ich bin gerächt*], so Kierkegaard is sensitive to the less than noble reality that often underlies the self-proclaimed virtues of his society.[46]

Among these numerous unmaskings, which deserve a separate essay, I shall mention only two. Though the present age is proud of its commitment to equality and to prudence, Kierkegaard finds these phenomena open to a very different interpretation that would make their bearers uncomfortable.

While Nietzsche finds resentment and revenge where people talk about justice, Kierkegaard finds envy barely hidden behind the praise of equality.[47] His polemic against equality is often so shrill as to be dismissed without being examined. In other writings he makes it clear that there is an equality that he affirms, grounded in the command of neighborly love. And in *Two Ages* he praises the Moravian Brethren for their religiously motivated pursuit of equality.[48] But he sees something entirely different in the leveling process by which mass society is constituted. Though this process is justified with the rhetoric of equality, we have already seen him (in the discussion of the herd as a sub-human society) suspect it of being the envy that demands that each should be just like the others.[49]

That earlier discussion of envy interpreted it in terms of an ontological difference between animal and spiritual existence. The particular animal is a specimen rather than an individual with a unique responsibility and destiny. As a printed reproduction is to an original painting, so is a particular animal to an individual human being. Envy is hostility directed against those who take their spiritual nature seriously enough to be anything but just like the others, anything but a social specimen. As such it is both a form of metaphysical rebellion, the flight from a spiritual vocation, and a form of intersubjectivity, "the *negatively unifying principle* in a passionless and very reflective age."[50]

---

[45]*TA*, 86; *PF*, 66-67; *WL*, 66.

[46]From "On the Virtuous" in *Thus Spake Zarathustra*. Cf. "On the Tarantulas." Both sections are from pt. 2. At this point Kierkegaard's method is more nearly *ad hominem* than before, like Hegel's method in the *Phenomenology*.

[47]*TA*, 84.

[48]*PV*, 118; *WL*, 70-72; *TA*, 66.

[49]Compare *JP*, 3:2986 (cited above, see n. 32) with 2:2166.

[50]*TA*, 81.

A negatively unifying principle is one that brings people together on the basis of what they are against, rather than what they support. The term *envy* suggests that what they are against in this case is difference. Kierkegaard offers a profound interpretation of this by noting an increasing unwillingness or inability to *admire* another. Since, as Marcel has noted, it is "the function of admiration to tear us away from ourselves and from the thoughts we have of ourselves," the envy that won't or can't admire is essentially egocentric. Kierkegaard draws the same connection and in the midst of his commentary on the demise of admiration he bluntly defines the leveling that springs from envy as selfishness.[51] While both love of the ideal and the love of neighbor place constraints on self-love, there is a love that does not, and thus can be easily put in the service of pure self-interest. This is the love of the crowd.[52]

The crucial test of this suggestion that the egalitarian sentiments of the modern age are instruments of self-interest (will to power), rather than commitments to the ideal of justice or compassion for the needy neighbor, would be to examine what happens to those sentiments when they lead in directions costly to the bearer. How does a union treat an individual who refuses to break the no-strike clause of a contract or public law? How does a bureaucracy respond to an individual who dares to blow the whistle on corruption or incompetence? What explanations are to be given of changing public attitudes toward social welfare and foreign-aid legislation? What happens to lofty statements about human rights and the folly of the arms race in the face of appeals to national interest and security? In short, is "liberty and justice for all" anything but a slogan? Once again Kierkegaard's critique suggests research projects for Socratic sociology.[53]

---

[51]Compare *TA,* 78-87 with Gabriel Marcel, *Creative Fidelity,* Robert Rosthal, trans. (New York: Farrer, Straus & Giroux, 1964) 47ff.

[52]*JP,* 2:1789, 1799, and *PV,* 118.

[53]It is clear that Kierkegaard's "Socratic Sociology" intends to be a critical theory of society. It thus invites comparison with the "critical theory" of the Frankfurt School, and of Jürgen Habermas in particular. It seems to me that the strongest affinity between the two lies in the centrality for both of what the comtemporary project calls *Ideologiekritik,* the attempt to unmask the false consciousness that emerges as society seeks to legitimate itself. See ch. 7 below. The two primary differences I see are these: First, Kierkegaard operates from explicitly normative premises (ethicoreligious), which he does not expect everyone to share and which he does not seek to derive from some unavoidable human interest. He would not be intimidated by the charge that his is a "moralizing" critique, a charge Habermas would consider devastating. Second, without denying the presence of coercion and unequal power in the contexts that generate false consciousness, Kierkegaard emphasizes the eager participation of the members of the herd in mass society and their willing acceptance of the self-deceptions necessary to validate their membership. Thus his kinship is more with Nietzsche than with Marx, though the difference between the socially weak and strong is even less important for him than for Nietzsche. See Raymond Geuss, *The Idea of*

Finally we come to an unmasking of prudence. In this case Kierkegaard finds laziness and even cowardice disguised as virtue. While the present age is proud of the calculating carefulness with which it weighs all the alternatives and avoids making a "big stupid blunder," he finds them to be *prudentially relaxing in indolence*" and "strangled by calculation." Though this age has great power at its disposal, and great skills of management, communication, transport, finance, and publicity, these are for the most part wasted, producing little that could be called action. This sluggishness is closely related to the previously noted boredom-entertainment syndrome. In sum, "Exhausted by its chimerical exertions, the present age then relaxes temporarily in complete indolence. Its condition is like that of the stay-abed in the morning who has big dreams, then torpor, followed by a witty or ingenious inspiration to excuse staying in bed. . . . *Vis inertiae* [the force of inertia] is at the bottom of the age's tergiversation."[54]

Cowardice and laziness parade as prudence. It takes no courage to side with the crowd against an individual. It may well be a cowardly act, as when the crowd spit on Jesus, though perhaps no one in the crowd would take personal responsibility for the act.[55] But the very essence of moral courage "is one person holding out alone, as a single individual, against the opposition of the numerical."[56] Here, as elsewhere, the question of courage is a question of fear. Moral courage is to fear God or to fear error more than one fears men, their laughter, or standing alone against them. Moral cowardice is the opposite.[57]

There are two elements in this cowardice. On the one hand, it is easy. Going the way of the group "makes life easier and more comfortable." But just because this path is the "coziest and most convenient, it is hypocritically prettied up to be true moral earnestness." The path of least resistance must be made to seem something better. Sometimes it masquerades as loyalty.[58] In *Two Ages* it is the pose of prudence that Kierkegaard seeks to expose with help, once again, from Socrates. Because Socrates feared God and error more than being alone against the crowd, he chose the right way instead of the easy way. Because his courage was matched by insight, he knew, and he helped

---

Critical Theory: Habermas and the Frankfurt School (New York: Cambridge University Press, 1981) and Thomas McCarthy, *The Critical Theory of Jürgen Habermas* (Cambridge: MIT Press, 1981).

[54]*TA,* 66-70, 94.

[55]*JP,* 3:2926, 2932, and *PV,* 113.

[56]*JP,* 3:2987.

[57]Ibid., 2:2162, 2166, 2171; 3:2941, 2976, 2988.

[58]Ibid., 4:4186; 3:2973, 2978.

us to see, that the easy way is sometimes the cowardly way posing as prudence.[59]

Traditionally prudence (self-control, temperance) was the rational control of the subrational. Kierkegaard and Socrates demonstrate that the rationalizing (legitimizing) of subrational behavior (laziness, cowardice) can also pass itself off as prudence. In this case the crucial test of whether prudence is rationality or rationalization can be formulated by two questions: Does prudence ever demand a strenuousness other than that of the rat race, in which I do my best to keep up with the crowd and climb a rung or two higher on its ladder? Does it ever call for the courage that says, as Socrates said to Athens, "Because of my loyalty to you I cannot but challenge the most basic assumptions of your lifeworld"? These questions imply that in the present age true prudence would show itself in radically countercultural behavior. At issue is not the counterculture of self-interest, which quietly folds its tents and evaporates when the draft is gone and drug laws are no longer strictly enforced. What is envisaged is rather the counterculture that springs from passionate commitment to the Idea and subjects both personal and social life to its critical scrutiny. To put it a bit more concretely, the issue is between the prudence that is expressed in the working principles of the military-industrial complex, which defines the world we live in, and the prudence that asks the deepest and most disturbing questions about what we think of as the most advanced civilization.

chapter

Abraham and Hegel

5

It has been rumored that Abraham will shortly receive an Oscar nomination for his supporting role in the greatest love story since Abelard and Heloise, that of Søren and Regina. If confirmed, these reports will come as no surprise since the placement of *Fear and Trembling* in its author's life is known to every reader of this dazzling but untimely meditation.

Reading this version of the Abraham story as a piece of spiritual autobiography may increase its lyrical intensity but does not illuminate its dialectical intrigue. For that illumination we must turn to another setting of the story, its place in the history of the Enlightenment. In its English, French, and German versions, deist and materialist, this movement erected an either/or between the Christian faith and reason, of which Lessing's "ugly, broad ditch" is perhaps the most vivid symbol.[1] The metaphysical and historical claims that lie at the heart of that faith were set aside as superstitions unacceptable to "modern man come of age."[2] Christian ethics were more or less spared, just as the leaders of victorious coups d'état often set up their headquarters in the palace of a deposed monarch.

The Enlightenment's triumph was ambiguous, however, for Romanticism emerged to express a hunger for the Infinite and Eternal that enlightened reason could not satisfy. Kant had been right in arguing that reason could only demand the Unconditioned, not achieve it.

But *Sehnsucht* is not salvation either, and Romanticism sank under the weight of its own sentimentality and irrationalism. The Enlightenment shrugged off the adolescent doubts of the Romantic interlude and recon-

---

[1]See "On the Proof of the Spirit and of Power," in *Lessing's Theological Writings,* Henry Chadwick, trans. (Stanford: Stanford University Press, 1957) and Kierkegaard's discussion in *CUP.*

[2]There is something ironic about the self-conscious modernity of the Enlightenment. For a thorough account of its equally self-conscious appeal to pagan antiquity, see Peter Gay, *The Rise of Modern Paganism,* vol. 1 of *The Enlightenment: An Interpretation* (New York: Random House, 1966).

quered much of the modern world, though not always with that faith in scientific reason that had swaddled the movement in its childhood. The heroes of this conquest do not all think alike, as a few names will suggest: Marx, Nietzsche, and Freud, Sartre and Camus, Russell and Carnap. Nevertheless, beyond their important differences they share a thorough confidence in the original either/or between religious faith and modernity and an equally uncompromising attitude toward any romantic mitigation of a world without grace.

This hurried history is neither original nor, I suspect, very controversial. It is incomplete, not just as any schematic account is bound to be, but essentially. It leaves out numerous attempts to negotiate a nonromantic compromise between the Enlightenment and Christian faith, of which Hegel's attempt to preserve the content of the latter in the form of the former is by far the most impressive. One of the most important features of the Hegelian synthesis is the quality of the opposition it attracted, most notably that of Marx and Kierkegaard. In the case of Kierkegaard the battle begins with brief skirmishes in *The Concept of Irony*. But in *Fear and Trembling,* the first full-scale battle is waged. We must turn to this conflict if we would fully appreciate the dialectical dexterity of Kierkegaard's storytelling.

Like David choosing five stones from the brook with which to face Goliath, Kierkegaard chooses a most unlikely weapon, Abraham. But this is not an arbitrary choice. If Christian faith is to show itself immune to Hegelian synthesis, why not focus on the one whom St. Paul presents in Romans 4 and Galatians 3 as the paradigm of faith and to whom Hebrews 11 gives more attention than anyone else in its catalogue of the heroes of faith? Why not stage a confrontation between Abraham and Hegel?

With Abraham's help, Kierkegaard plans a double assault on the central thesis of Hegel's mature speculation, to which the opening five paragraphs of the *Encyclopedia* are devoted. That would be the claim that Hegel's philosophy contains the same content as the Christian religion, but in the superior form of philosophical concept, *Begriff,* rather than the religious form Hegel labels *Vorstellung*. Kierkegaard's first challenge will be to the supremacy of the concept, the second to the identity of content.[3]

I

It is supposed to be difficult to understand Hegel, but to understand Abraham is a trifle. To go beyond Hegel is a miracle, but to get beyond Abraham is the easiest thing of all.[4]

---

[3]In the same year that *FT* appeared Feuerbach raised these same two issues in his preface to the second edition of *The Essence of Christianity*. See *The Fiery Brook: Selected Writings of Ludwig Feuerbach,* Zawar Hanfi, trans. (Garden City: Doubleday, 1972) 248-49. The crucial passages are omitted from the standard English edition.

[4]*FT,* 32-33.

The first issue emerges in the preface and epilogue, which form a satirical frame for retelling the Abraham story. In both, the idea of going beyond faith is scathingly pilloried.[5] The preface suggests that by this means, Christianity is reduced to such a bargain price that there are no longer any customers; while the epilogue recounts the story of the Holland spice merchants who dumped several cargoes into the sea to peg up prices and offers this as a model for what might be needed in the realm of the spirit. In other words, Kierkegaard (via Johannes de Silentio, the pseudonym) will try to present faith as a more costly commodity than those who have gone further would take it to be. After all, doesn't Jesus teach in the Gospels that the Kingdom is like a pearl of great price for which one would sell everything else? Such a pearl is surely not to be found in the bargain basement or at the local discount center.[6]

In the midst of his satirical forays, Johannes remains serious enough to present us with his own idea of what faith really is, the task of a lifetime and the highest passion in a man. Of the first he writes, "In our time nobody is content to stop with faith but wants to go further. It would perhaps be rash to ask where these people are going, but it is surely a sign of breeding and culture for me to assume that everybody has faith, for otherwise it would be queer for them to be . . . going further. In those old days it was different, then faith was a task for a whole lifetime, because it was assumed that dexterity in faith is not acquired in a few days or weeks."[7]

The Abraham picture itself must show concretely how faith could be a lifetime task, but the frame presents us with two analogies, doubting and loving. Modern philosophy begins with doubt, but of course quickly goes further.[8] This is surely a bargain-basement doubt compared to that of the "ancient Greeks (who also had some understanding of philosophy)" who viewed doubt as "a task of a whole lifetime, seeing that dexterity in doubting is not acquired in a few days or weeks."[9] Today we might have chosen the Vedantist or the Buddhist as an example, since Kierkegaard is following Hegel's notion here that the truly philosophical skepticism is not a Humean or positivist skepti-

---

[5]In addition to the passage cited above, this theme is alluded to in numerous passages outside the preface and epilogue. See *FT*, 9, 22-23, 37, 50-51, 69, 115.

[6]Matt. 13:45-46. Kierkegaard complains that the Christianity of Christendom has become "a superficial something which neither wounds nor heals profoundly enough" (*TC*, 139).

[7]*FT*, 7. His ellipsis. On life as a gift and a task, see the critique of romantic irony in *CI*, 293ff. For an autobiographical account of what Kierkegaard understood by the concept of a task, see *EO*, 2:271ff.

[8]In the year before he wrote *FT* Kierkegaard began but did not finish or publish an essay on doubt and modern philosophy. It is available to us as *JC*.

[9]*FT*, 7.

cism but one that comes to see "the given" as most highly problematical.[10] Such doubt is not a casual or temporary project, but an endless task so long as one has not yet left the human condition and, to use the Eastern examples, passed over into undifferentiated union with Brahman or into Nirvana.[11]

The other analogy is from the epilogue. Love is the task of a lifetime. The one who has reached faith "does not remain standing at faith, yea, he would be offended if anyone were to say this of him, just as the lover would be indignant if one said that he remained standing at love, for he would reply, 'I do not remain standing by any means, my whole life is in this.' Nevertheless he does not get further." Why not? Because the seriousness of the task of loving lies in its "authentically human factor," passion. "Thus no generation has learned from another to love."[12]

In that significant "Thus" we are reminded of the way the preface contrasts passion with learning. The point is not to suggest that reflection is necessarily dispassionate, but to protest the way in which the age has made it so by its commitment to objectivity.[13] At the same time we are reminded that what is essential to love (and faith) is an element of passion that is neither reducible to nor deducible from any form of learning, the theoretical learning of the learned or the practical learning of the socialized. Love is not *Bildung*, nor is faith, and God has no grandchildren. Satire aside for the moment, Johannes turns hortatory. "But the highest passion in a man is faith, and here no generation begins at any other point than did the preceding generation, every

---

[10]See the essay of 1802 entitled *Verhältniss des Skepticismus zur Philosophie* and the echoes of it in paragraph 39 of the *Encyclopedia* and the *Zusätze* to paragraphs 24 and 81. The Logic of the *Encyclopedia* is often referred to as the "Lesser Logic." Subsequent references to it will be by LL and paragraph (not page) numbers, which are common to all editions. References to the *Encyclopedia*'s Philosophy of Spirit will be by PS and paragraph number. Z signifies the *Zusatz* to the designated paragraph. I have followed the Wallace and Miller translations respectively.

[11]Implicitly challenged here is the transition to the Hegelian system from the *Phenomenology*. We will be prepared for the ether of the former by passing over the phenomenological highway of doubt and despair in which our confidence in the ordinary deliverances of consciousness is shaken. The doubt that is prerequisite for faith Kierkegaard calls irony and infinite resignation. It "rescues the soul from the snares of relativity" (*CI*, 113). Phenomenological doubt is similarly a prerequisite for Hegelian speculation. Hegel stresses the difficulty of this path, but it is so far from being the task of a lifetime that the system presupposes its achievement. By contrast Kierkegaard makes suffering an essential determination of faith insofar as faith involves the perpetual, lifelong task of dying to immediacy. See *CUP*, 386-448.

[12]*FT*, 121-22.

[13]Ibid., 7. Cf. 27, 42n, 67, and the suggestion on 9 that if only he were a learned exegete of Hebrew he would understand Abraham. In *CUP*, 313 and 176-177, Kierkegaard develops the formula that existence plus reflection produces passion, and he stresses passion as a crucial element in what he calls "essential knowledge."

generation begins all over again, the subsequent generation gets no further than the foregoing. . . . If the generation would only concern itself about its task, which is the highest thing it can do, it cannot grow weary, for the task is always sufficient for a human life. . . . Faith is the highest passion in a man. There are perhaps many in every generation who do not even reach it, but no one gets further."[14]

Since Hegel clearly viewed his thought as the culmination of a development spanning many generations, it looks as if there is a fundamental difference between faith, as understood by Kierkegaard, and philosophy, as understood by Hegel. Doubt is prerequisite to both, but in strikingly different ways, and philosophy benefits from the achievements of preceding generations, while faith does not. But Hegel too affirms that religious faith and philosophical wisdom are significantly different—in form though not in content. What needs to be shown now is that Kierkegaard's polemic against going beyond faith is a critique not just of the *Phenomenology*'s relation to the system,[15] but also of the more important Hegelian theory of the relation between religious *Vorstellungen* and philosophical *Begriffe*. Its intention to be such a critique is overt. Johannes writes in the preface, "Even though one were capable of converting the whole content of faith into the form of a concept, it does not follow that one has adequately conceived faith and understands how one got into it or how it got into one."[16]

Two misunderstandings must be avoided if the issue is to be sharply focused. First notice that in the passage before us Kierkegaard does not present the truism that faith is not understanding. Nor does he challenge the idea that faith should seek understanding. The question is whether, in reflecting on its content or object, faith also comes to an understanding of itself, or rather loses sight of itself. Kierkegaard prefers Socratic to Hegelian dialectic because the former never neglects the Delphic command, "Know thyself," while the latter commits precisely this sin, in what the *Postscript* calls a world-historical fit of absentmindedness. Such, at any rate, is the allegation.

We might say that Hegelian reflection is faith seeking to understand God, while Kierkegaardian reflection is faith seeking to understand itself. After all, it is of Abraham and not God that Johannes writes, "No one is so great as [he]! Who is capable of understanding him?"[17] However, that would be to misrepresent Kierkegaard's point, which is not to direct our attention away from God but toward Him so as to realize that a proper knowledge of this "object" must

---

[14]*FT*, 121-22. Quickly returning to the satirical mood, Johannes concludes with a reference to the disciple of Heraclitus who went beyond his master by reverting to the Eleatic thesis that motion was impossible.

[15]See n. 11.

[16]*FT*, 7.

[17]Ibid., 14.

involve the knower's "infinite, personal, passionate interest" in his own relation to what is known. This knowing can be called essential knowledge because it is essentially related to the knower's own personal existence. It belongs to a context in which the properly conceived *what* is useless if the *how* is inappropriate. For what shall it profit us if we comprehend God comprehensively but fail to trust and obey him?[18]

The other misunderstanding would be to confuse the issue here with that between Hegel and the philosophies of immediacy (Jacobi, Schleiermacher, etc.). The possibility of such a misunderstanding lies in two facts. Kierkegaard speaks of faith as an immediacy and Hegel speaks of knowledge as mediation. In doing the latter Hegel uses the very language of going beyond that the frame satire employs. Objects can be given to consciousness in many ways, but to reflect upon them is to go beyond their givenness. Thus every form of thought involves "the negation of what we have immediately before us." It is this negative movement that is called mediation. "For to mediate is to take something as a beginning and to go onward to something else."[19]

From his critique of Jacobi in *Glauben und Wissen* (1802) and throughout his life Hegel felt the need to defend philosophy as mediating thought against an appeal to immediacy, which he took to be a virulent disease of the spirit. The time and energy he devoted to opposing it suggest that he saw it as having assumed epidemic proportions. It is, briefly, the romantic solution to the Kantian dilemma. We demand the Unconditioned, but reason—understood here as mediating thought in all its forms—is unable to provide us with it.

------

[18]Cf. *CUP*, 33 and the whole discussion of truth as subjectivity. In *CUP* and *CD* Kierkegaard constantly worries about the question of the appropriate mode for discourse about God. Among the indications that this issue is already at work in *FT* are (1) that the section entitled "Preliminary Expectoration" is framed by a satirical but plainly serious discussion of how and how not to preach about Abraham (*FT*, 27-30 and 52-53) and (2) that Johannes worries elsewhere about speaking humanly and inhumanly about his theme (*FT*, 34 and 64). Closely related to Kierkegaard's thought here is Luther's distinction between true knowledge of God and self, in which one actually experiences one's own sinfulness, and "speculative" knowledge, in which this does not occur. See the 1535 *Lectures on Galatians* in vol. 26 of *Luther's Works*, Jaroslav Pelikan, ed. (St. Louis: Concordia, 1963) 131, 148, 288 and the discussion of Psalm 51 in vol. 12 (1955) 310ff., 385, and 403. The difference between Kierkegaard and Hegel on this point is partially expressed by the fact that the former sharply distinguishes worship from comprehension, while the latter sees philosophy and worship as the same. Compare *TC*, 139 with Hegel's *Lectures on the Philosophy of Religion*, Spiers and Sanderson, trans. (New York: Humanities, 1962) 1:20. Where paragraph numbers are not at hand for Hegel's works, references will also be given to the German texts, as found in *Werke in Zwanzig Bänden* (Frankfurt: Suhrkamp, 1969), according to the following abbreviations: *Religion*, 1:20 = *Werke*, 16:28. I have felt free to modify existing translations slightly without mention.

[19]*LL*, 12.

Rather than draw a positivist conclusion from the first *Critique*, the alternative is to claim a direct, noninferential, even nonconceptual prehension of the Infinite and Eternal. We could again avail ourselves of Vedantist or Buddhist analogies were it not for the fact that instead of portraying this immediate awareness of the Absolute as the result of a long and arduous discipline, it is presented as given with the same primordial obviousness as that with which we experience, for example, our own bodies.

There is no need to elaborate on the details of Hegel's polemic against this view.[20] The important point is that although Hegel regularly speaks of faith as an immediacy and the movement from *Vorstellung* to *Begriff* as mediation, he consistently portrays religious faith as thoroughly mediated and only relatively immediate. The thrust of his argument, then, is that one mode of mediation requires another, relative to which the first has a kind of immediacy. This is quite different from refuting an appeal to pure immediacy as the only legitimate "knowledge" of God.

There are, for Hegel, two senses in which even a prespeculative knowledge of God is mediated. God is not, like the objects of other sciences, among the "natural admissions of consciousness."[21] To have faith in God is to rise above and beyond the sensible world that empiricism allows as given to consciousness. This elevation (*Erhebung*) is at once the essence of faith and a paradigm of mediation.[22]

Corresponding to this logical mediation is the psychological process that Hegel calls *Bildung*. The ideas we have of God are not innate but actually the result of a long and gradual process of training and socialization. *Der gebildete Mensch* has a mind whose contents have not been left in their natural state but humanized through the educational process.[23]

---

[20]There are five main points to the critique. (1) Strictly speaking, there is no such thing as immediate knowledge, for knowledge implies content, while a purely immediate awareness would be entirely indeterminate, void of any content whatever. (2) Since one's principle is devoid of content, it is entirely arbitrary what eventually gets affirmed as immediately given. The certainty and self-evidence claimed for immediacy are no guarantee of truth whatever. (3) Since the truth is to be determined by the unchecked subjectivity of private opinion, there is a socially anarchist implication to this philosophy. (4) Paradoxically, there is an uncritical conservatism as the usual result, for what is self-evident is most likely to be what is traditional and familiar. (5) Since immediacy has been appealed to on behalf of religious ideas that reason had been unable to support, it must be noted that the Christian religion always has something quite different in mind when it speaks of faith, for it always affirms a specific content and an authority beyond that of private certainty.

[21]"*unmittelbar von der Vorstellung zugegeben,*" LL, 1.

[22]Ibid., 12 and *Religion*, 1:166 = *Werke*, 16:161.

[23]*LL*, 67; *Religion*, 1:74, 132-34 = *Werke*, 16:78-79, 130-31; *Lectures on the Proofs of the Existence of God* (henceforth *Proofs*), in *Religion*, 3:177 = *Werke*, 17:368-69.

In the same logical and psychological senses religious faith is relatively immediate. When it is not meant as a polemic against further reflection, Hegel even accepts the idea that the consciousness of God is immediately given with consciousness of the self, that is, that its status is the same as that of the *cogito*. While in neither case, that of the self nor of God, does Hegel permit this to preclude further discussion as to their nature, it seems that there is at least a formal sense in which he wants to make awareness of the Infinite transcendental in the Cartesian and Kantian sense. Even the concrete contents of religious consciousness come to have the kind of self-evidence that gives them the logical priority of presuppositions or assumptions. Hegel speaks of them, in this capacity as functionally a priori, as an "unconscious immediacy."[24]

To call this logical priority functional is to say that it derives from a sociopsychological familiarity. *Bildung* is not only a process; it is also a result, which Hegel refers to as *gewöhnliches* or *gemeines Bewusstsein*.[25] Our ideas of God are thus *zunächst* in the form of *Vorstellung, zuletzt* in that of *Begriff*.[26] Philosophy is often discredited through a *Sehnsucht nach einer bereits bekannten, geläufigen Vorstellung*.[27] It is just this familiarity that transforms the results of complicated mediations into the immediacy of self-evidence. So in religious consciousness we are dealing with "a result which at once does away with itself as result." It "is in a state of constant unrest between immediate sensuous perception on the one hand and thought proper on the other." While I can believe in God, I cannot in that sense believe that there is a sky above me or that the Pythagorean theorem is true. Faith falls between the immediacy of sensible presentness and the mediation that yields rational necessity.[28]

The immediacy of religious consciousness for Hegel is thus quite distinct from the immediacy to which Jacobi appeals. Correspondingly, his case for the need to move from *Vorstellung* to *Begriff* is different from his polemic against romantic philosophies of feeling and intuition. There is no misunderstanding on Kierkegaard's part. In *The Concept of Irony* and in *Either/Or* Kierkegaard presents a thoroughly Hegelian critique of the romantic subjectivism that Hegel finds implicit in the appeal to immediacy. More important, when he speaks of faith as a second immediacy, distinct from any "aesthetic emotion" or "immediate instinct of the heart" and subsequent to the move-

---

[24]*Religion*, 1:43, 116, 119 = *Werke*, 16:49, 115, 118, and *Proofs*, 3:160-61 = *Werke*, 17:353.

[25]*LL*, 3, 4, and 6, and *Proofs*, 3:203 = *Werke*, 17:391.

[26]*LL*, 2; *Proofs*, 3:203 = *Werke*, 17:392; *Religion*, 1:116 = *Werke*, 16:115.

[27]*LL*, 3. Cf. *LL*, 66 and the preface to the *Phenomenology*, which also contains a penetrating critique of the allegedly immediate as the merely familiar.

[28]*Religion*, 1:65, 117, 145 = *Werke*, 16:70, 116, 141.

ment of infinite resignation, he too affirms that whatever immediacy faith involves is relative and permeated with mediation.[29]

What we have to consider, then, is not Hegel's general thesis that every mode of life and thought involves mediation,[30] but the special thesis that the richly mediated position of religious faith, which comes to have a functional immediacy, requires a further mediation in which *Vorstellung* is replaced by *Begriff*. Furthermore, we must consider this thesis in the light of Kierkegaard's concern that knowledge of God should involve the knower's existence.

The additional mediation that speculation provides is necessary because while religion offers us our earliest acquaintance with what is also a subject of philosophy, namely God as Truth, that acquaintance is "inadequate." It is only when this content has been transformed from *Vorstellung* to *Begriff* or *Gedanke* that it is "for the first time put in its proper light."[31] Contaminated by the accretion of elements that do not properly belong to it, it stands in need of the "purification" that only this new mediation can provide.[32] Philosophy therefore takes up a polemic stance toward the form of religious consciousness.[33] In the course of following this polemic, the differences between *Vorstellung* and *Begriff* as Hegel understands them will come to light.

---

[29]*FT,* 47, 69, 82-83. Cf. *SLW,* 364 and *JP,* 2:1123, where Kierkegaard writes (in 1848) that "faith is immediacy or spontaneity after reflection." In an earlier entry (from 1836, 2:1096), he writes, "What Schleiermacher calls 'religion' and the Hegelian dogmaticians 'faith' is, after all, nothing else than the first immediacy, the prerequisite for everything—the vital fluid—in an emotional-intellectual sense the atmosphere we breathe—and which therefore cannot properly be characterized with these words [faith and religion]." We have seen that this would be a mistaken reading of Hegel, and Kierkegaard does not level this charge against either Hegel or his own contemporaries in *FT*. It is *Bildung* and not the first immediacy that he finds them confusing with faith.

[30]"[T]here is nothing, nothing in heaven or in nature or mind or anywhere else which does not equally contain both immediacy and mediation, so that these two determinations reveal themselves to be *unseparated* and inseparable." *Hegel's Science of Logic,* A. V. Miller, trans. (London: George Allen & Unwin, 1969) 68 = *Wissenschaft der Logik,* Georg Lasson, ed. (Hamburg: Felix Meiner, 1967 1:52. Cf. *Proofs,* 3:175 = *Werke,* 17:367.

[31]*LL,* 1 and 5.

[32]*Proofs,* 3:201-202 = *Werke,* 17:391.

[33]The polemic is, if anything, more vehement in the *Phenomenology*. Page references will be given first to the Miller translation (Oxford: Clarendon Press, 1977) and then to the Hoffmeister edition (Hamburg: Felix Meiner, 1952). We read that *Vorstellung* is an imperfect form, in which the mediation process is incomplete and which manifests a defect in the connection between thought and being. Consequently, for the true content to attain the true form, it is necessary to attain *die höhere Bildung* of the concept (462-63 = 531-32). At the level of *Vorstellung* the content of faith is degraded (*herabsetzen,* 466 = 535). Its understanding of the Incarnation is an "impov-

Though he usually names the religious form of consciousness simply as *Vorstellung,* Hegel subdivides its modes for a more detailed analysis. When he does this he distinguishes three moments of faith: *Gefühl* or *Fühlen, Anschauung,* and *Vorstellung.* Feeling is an important element in religion because in feeling the divine is given to us with certainty, and the unity with what is other is directly experienced. *Was mir ein Anderes ist, vermeinige ich.* But feeling cannot be the only element in religion. At this level God loses both the content and the independent reality that religion affirms, for, since feeling is prior to the subject-object distinction, it is a unity without difference.[34]

Perception is treated only very briefly. *Anschauung* immediately becomes *Kunstanschauung,* and Hegel seems to have in mind the mythological religion of ancient Greece that he so loves to discuss. The critique is simple. In this mode the divine becomes an object of consciousness and gains the determinateness and objectivity that pure feeling could not provide, but it does so in an unqualifiedly sensible way inappropriate to the sacred. As in the previous case, Hegel intends this critique to be one that Christian faith would join him in making.[35]

It is only in the discussion of *Vorstellung* proper that the debate between Hegel and Kierkegaard comes into focus. To each of Hegel's major points Kierkegaard's reply is the same. His reply is an invitation to put Abraham through the "purification" Hegel proposes to see whether what washes away is unessential or Abraham himself. Kierkegaard speaks through Johannes de Silentio, the satirist turned lawyer-for-the-defense.

1. To distinguish *Vorstellung* proper from *Anschauung* Hegel begins by stressing that it is not the mode of pure image *(Bild).* As thought, it has a universality and an objectivity that surpass imagination. Although it is negative toward the sensible, it is not fully freed from it. Separating itself from the sensible, *Vorstellung* becomes abstract and thereby dependent on sense images for determination. This involves religion in its analogical use of such terms as son, begetting, wrath, repentance, and vengeance, in which the palpably human is attributed to God, though not literally. This is an unstable position between sense perception and authentic thought that frees itself from all dependence on sense.[36]

---

erishment of Spirit" and the "non-spiritual recollection of a supposed individual figure and of its past" (463 = 533). It is thereby reduced to "an incomprehensible happening . . . in the form of *indifferent being*" (471 = 541). Self-knowledge is not really possible at this level, nor can truth be at one with certainty (477, 485 = 547, 556). By contrast with *Wissenschaft,* the perfect form of spirit's self-knowledge, religious consciousness is "uncultivated," "harsh," and "barbarous" (488 = 559).

[34]*Religion,* 1:118-38 = *Werke,* 16:117-35.

[35]Ibid., 1:138-41 = 16:135-38.

[36]Ibid., 1:142-45 = 16:139-42.

And Johannes: "But what is left of my Abraham? His faith presupposes that God is the giver and keeper of promises, one who can be trusted and who must be obeyed. The absolute trust of Abraham is the highest passion we can have and to learn his sort of obedience is the task of a lifetime. But now I am told that talk of God as giver and keeper of promises is too sense bound and that we must go beyond this to a more purely categoreal vocabulary. What then happens to the passion and the task? What is left of my Abraham?"

2. For Hegel, the historical as such belongs to *Vorstellung* as well. Though we take the history of Jesus Christ to be history and not myth, the same task of finding "the inward, the true, the substantial element" of the narrative—that is, of distinguishing the meaning from the external form—applies to historical as well as mythical texts. The trouble with *Vorstellung* is that it portrays the divine action, "divine, timeless events," as if they were historical events.[37]

And Johannes: "What is left of my Abraham? The divine acts on which his trust is grounded are no 'timeless events,' but the very particular and temporal experiences of coming to Canaan and having a son in his old age. Nor is the demand that he offer up his son a timeless truth. Its entirely sudden eruption into his life evokes tremendous passion, and learning to live with such a God is surely the task of a lifetime. But if God's activity is to be understood as timeless events, what happens to the passion and the task? What is left of my Abraham?"

3. In contrast with feeling, which expresses unity without difference, *Vorstellung* expresses difference with insufficient unity. For example, when creation is studied at this level of thought, the relation of God to the world has a contingency and externality quite distinct from the necessity required by speculative thought.[38]

And Johannes: "But you simply haven't been listening. If God's relation to the world is transformed into rational necessity the situation is changed beyond recognition. Given a rational necessity to God's requirement we would still have a passionate Abraham. But his would be the passion of a tragic hero, not of the knight of faith. Not everyone can be a tragic hero, for it is no simple task to learn infinite resignation in the face of impersonal fate. But then it is not the task of a lifetime either. What is left of my Abraham?"

4. At the level of the philosophical concept "the givenness, the authority, and externality of the content over against me vanish." What was dark and impenetrable becomes transparent. In both these respects the Platonic the-

---

[37]Ibid., 1:146 = 16:142. Cf. 156 = 152.

[38]Ibid., 1:147-48 = 16:143-44. Cf. *LL*, 1 and *Proofs*, 3:201-202 = *Werke*, 17:391.

ory of recollection becomes the appropriate model for our knowledge of God. Thought can be entirely free and self-sufficient because the truth is within us.[39]

And Johannes: "It seems I can't get through. It is just because the authority of God's command remains so dark and impenetrable that Abraham's passion is raised to a peak. And to describe how Abraham might have gotten himself into this predicament via Platonic recollection—*that* would be the task of a lifetime if it were not so patently foolish. When nothing is commanded and everything is clear, what is left of my Abraham?"

5. While the previous point grows out of the third, since rational necessity is the best candidate for the kind of truth that is within us, the present point is a corollary of the fourth. As authority is replaced by rational necessity, the paraenetic character of discourse about God is lost. "It is not the purpose of philosophy to edify." Philosophy can presuppose the existence of faith and therefore need not concern itself with evoking faith. Of course, philosophy recognizes that in the realm of human freedom what is and what ought to be do not always coincide, and that there are individuals who through self-will, perversity, indolence, and obstinacy stand outside the truth; but "the fact is no man is so utterly ruined, so lost, and so bad, nor can we regard any one as being so wretched that he has no religion whatever in him, even if it were only that he has the fear of it, or some yearning after it, or a feeling of hatred towards it." For this reason we can say that though some are ungodly "it is not, however, the aim of knowledge to lead to piety, nor is it meant to do so." The task of the concept is to comprehend whatever religion does exist.[40]

And Johannes: "You say that philosophy must beware of the wish to be edifying. I say the Jutland pastor was right when he preached that 'only the truth which edifies is truth for you.' I have always said that 'the thing is to find a truth which is true *for me*, to find *the idea for which I can live and die*. . . . What good would it do me if truth stood before me, cold and naked, not caring whether I recognized her or not. . . . What is truth but to live for an idea?'[41] I am no philosopher. I surely don't understand the System and I probably don't

---

[39]*Religion*, 1:155, 165 = *Werke*, 16:151, 160. Cf. *LL*, 4; *Religion*, 1:2-3 = *Werke*, 16:12-13; *Proofs*, 3:161 = *Werke*, 17:353. From this point of view it is no accident that the idea of the paradox and of the absurd, so central to *PF*, is already introduced in *FT*. As early as *CI*, 67-68, Kierkegaard had expressed his distrust of the recollection model. "As Socrates so beautifully binds mankind firmly to the divine by showing that all knowledge is recollection, so Plato . . ." Beautifully? Yes, but not finally tenable, even for Socrates, who ends up ignorant.

[40]*Religion*, 1:4-6 = *Werke*, 16:14-15. Cf. LL, 6 on philosophy's attitude toward "is" and "ought," and the preface to the *Phenomenology*, where Hegel first wrote, "But philosophy must beware of the wish to be edifying" (6 = 14).

[41]The line from the Jutland pastor is the last line of *EO*. The other quotations are from Kierkegaard's often-quoted Gilleleie journal of August 1835. See *The Journals of Kierkegaard*, Alexander Dru, trans. (New York: Harper & Row, 1959) 44-45.

even understand Kant. But ever since I read him at the university I have been moved by the heart of his great Critique, the Transcendental Deduction. The transcendental unity of apperception is justified as a first principle of knowledge because without it the content of my knowledge and experience would not be mine. This seemed to me the truly revolutionary theme in Kant, that philosophical reflection primarily concerns itself with the conditions under which the various contents of experience can be mine.[42] It seemed to me that Kant went about this in a highly abstract and formal way, and when I first heard how philosophy had gone beyond Kant I was thrilled, especially since it was clear that knowledge of the Infinite and Eternal was no longer to be excluded. But then I read that philosophy must beware of the wish to be edifying, and I realized that reflection was trying to divest itself of its natural passion, and that philosophy had gone beyond Kant by leaving out his most important insight. I was reminded of the disciple of Heraclitus who went beyond his master by reverting to the Eleatic thesis which denies movement.[43]

"When you said that philosophy presupposes the existence of faith I at first began to smile. For when Abraham is taken as the paradigm of faith it is comically preposterous for any philosophy, especially a presuppositionless philosophy, to presuppose the existence of faith in its hearers. But you went right on to indicate that the faith you presuppose is somewhat less rigorous and that even a feeling of hatred toward religion will count as faith so far as the concept is concerned (or should I say unconcerned). Then I began to wonder. Suppose Abraham had come by faith to Canaan and by faith had received a son in his old age, but then, seeing that he had but little time left, had gone beyond faith to the concept. He would have learned that when the truth is purified of its inadequacies and seen for the first time in its proper light it is less concerned than he had thought about his trusting and obeying. He would have learned that the Truth was quite distinct from the God with whom he had been in covenant. No doubt Abraham would have enjoyed a relaxation from the strenuousness of faith, but what would be left of my Abraham?"

6. It is time to consider a feature of Hegel's position that has not come to light in the discussion so far. There are passages that indicate that he is no more enthusiastic for a philosophy without a heart than he is for a faith without understanding. "Philosophic thought and religious faith are part of a liv-

---

[42]"It must be possible for the 'I think' to accompany all my representations; for otherwise something would be represented in me which could not be thought at all, and that is equivalent to saying that the representation would be impossible, or at least would be nothing to me. . . . For the manifold representations, which are given in an intuition, would not be one and all *my* representations, if they did not all belong to one self-consciousness." *Critique of Pure Reason*, B 131-32.

[43]*FT*, 123.

ing whole, *each fragmentary by itself*."[44] The *Vorstellungen* of faith are "metaphors" of philosophical concepts. One can have the metaphor without understanding its meaning for thought, but the converse is also true. "It is one thing to have *Gedanken* and *Begriffe*, and another to know what *Vorstellungen, Anschauungen,* and *Gefühle* correspond to them."[45] On the other hand, the two modes of consciousness can accompany one another, and in fact it is necessary that they do so.[46] The reason for this necessity is that the content must become "identical with me" until I am "so penetrated through and through with it that it constitutes my qualitative, determinate character. . . . It thus becomes my feeling." This does not guarantee its truth, but it does mean that the content "makes itself actively felt in the life of the individual and governs his entire conduct, active and passive."[47]

In other words, "We must have God in our heart." This is not a matter of momentary feelings but of the "continuous, permanent manner of my existence *(Existenz)*" that we call character. For when we speak of God it is clear that "I, as actual, as this definite individual, am to be determined through and through by this content." *Der gebildete Mensch* is one whose heart and feelings have been humanized by the influence of reason and thought and, conversely, whose mind is not dissociated from his character.[48]

Perhaps Johannes has been a bit hasty in his complaint that "it is dishonest of philosophy to give something else instead of [faith] and to make light of faith. . . . Least of all should [philosophy] fool people out of something as if it were nothing."[49] Particularly in his various lectures on religion, Hegel seems to hold that faith is by no means nothing and that, while it is something distinct from philosophy, it is no less an important element of *Bildung* than philosophy is. Whether or not this will satisfy Johannes we will have to hear from his own lips.

And Johannes: "So you think we need to have God in our hearts after all. While I do not profess myself to be a man of Abraham's faith, I am glad to hear you say this, but am at a loss to reconcile it with your polemic against the religious form of consciousness. If the link between my life and my ideas of God is so all important as you say should it not be to the inadequacy of the concept which reflection calls attention? Can there really be any sense to the idea that only at the level of *Begriffe*, where this link has been systematically

---

[44]Quoted from a Berlin review of a book by C. F. Goeschel in Emil Fackenheim, *The Religious Dimension in Hegel's Thought* (Bloomington: Indiana University Press, 1967) 192. My italics.

[45]*LL*, 3. Cf. *Religion,* 1:24-25 = *Werke,* 16:32-33.

[46]*Proofs,* 3:164 = *Werke,* 17:356 and *Religion,* 1:132 = *Werke,* 16:130.

[47]*Proofs,* 3:180-81 = *Werke,* 17:372-73 and *Religion,* 1:4 = *Werke,* 16:13. Cf. 7 = 16.

[48]*Religion,* 1:133ff. = *Werke,* 16:131ff.

[49]*FT,* 33.

cut, as we seem to agree, do our ideas of God appear in their "proper light"? From what point of view is the abstraction from this "existential" dimension, to coin a phrase, a "purification" from the unessential. It seems to me that your reflection is governed by the ideal of Aristotle's knight of intellectual virtue, while mine is trying to come to grips with Abraham as the knight of faith. I know that Aristotle portrays pure contemplation, theoria, as the most divine activity, but that hardly fits the God who called and tested Abraham and who sent his Son into the world to save it; and in any case, I've always assumed that the task was to be human. But now we're touching on another subject. To ask what conception of God is presupposed by your exaltation of *Begriff* above *Vorstellung* is to go beyond the question of form to the question of content. I am about to express my suspicion that the content of your philosophical speculation is not the same as that of the Christian religion, in spite of your claim that it is."[50]

II

How often have I shown that fundamentally Hegel makes men into heathens, *into a race of animals gifted with reason*. For in the animal world "the individual" is always less important than the race. But it is the peculiarity of the human race that just because the individual is created in the image of God "the individual" is above the race.

This can be wrongly understood and terribly misused: *concedo*. But that is Christianity. And *that* is where the battle must be fought.[51]

We have been considering the frame. We must turn now to the picture itself, the retelling of the Abraham story, where Johannes's doubts about the identity of content come to the fore. He proceeds by posing three questions about the story, whose discussion makes up the body of his little book. Hegel is mentioned by name at the beginning of each of these discussions and the confrontation between Abraham and Hegel intensifies. Each time the structure is the same; the ethical is understood as the universal. If this is the ultimate framework for human existence, then the Hegelian philosophy is correct on this or that central theme, but in such a way that consistency would require Hegel to renounce Abraham as a murderer rather than honor him as the father of the faithful. On the other hand, the kind of faith that Abraham ex-

---

[50]Hegel's Aristotelian priority of intellectual over moral virtue receives a variety of expressions. In n. 18 above, his identification of philosophy with worship has already been noted. In *The Philosophy of History* (henceforth *History*), J. Sibree, trans. (New York: Dover, 1956), he writes, "The *ne plus ultra* [*die letzte Spitze*] of inwardness is thought" (439 = *Werke*, 12:521). In *Proofs* he goes further, first identifying thought and inwardness, then proceeding to describe thinking reason, the essence of the human spirit, as itself divine (3:157-58 = *Werke*, 17:349-50). Cf. *Religion*, 1:33 = *Werke*, 16:40.

[51]*The Journals of Kierkegaard*, 187. His italics. Cf. *FT*, 55-56 and *SUD*, 83.

hibits requires that the individual, in relation to God, be higher than the universal. If this be not the case, Abraham is lost.[52]

The point is clear. No one claims that Abraham is a philosopher. But if Hegelian philosophy requires that he no longer be honored as the father of faith, this could only be because, in content as well as form, it differs from the Christian faith of the New Testament, which holds up Abraham as a prototype of our true relation to God.

It is important to consider seriously that Hegel and not Kant is under scrutiny. To call the ethical the universal in the Kantian context means that moral principles have a priori status—the universal validity that derives from rational necessity—and that as such they are unexceptionable. This is not the issue between Kierkegaard and Hegel; for whatever type of rational necessity moral principles have for Hegel, it does not mean that they are unexceptionable. The tragic heroes whom Kierkegaard presents—Agamemnon, Jephtha, and Brutus—remain comfortably within the framework of the universal although they teleologically suspend their duty to their children and slay them. Since this is not the teleological suspension of the ethical that Kierkegaard describes, it is clear that his target is not Kant's essay "On the Supposed Right to Lie from Altruistic Motives."

It is another universality that defines the ethical in the Hegelian scheme, the concrete universality of the social order. Kierkegaard explicitly identifies the universal he has in mind as being the nation, the state, the laws, society, a people.[53] Agamemnon, Jephtha, and Brutus remain within the ethical because they teleologically suspend the lesser universality of family responsibilities for the greater universality of the nation. In Hegelian terms, then, the universality of the ethical designates not *Moralität*, with its inner conviction

---

[52]In the third discussion the description of Abraham's being lost does not come in the opening paragraphs but at 113 and 120. Though Kierkegaard could not have known it, Hegel did write a very bitter polemic against Abraham. It belongs to the essay we know as "The Spirit of Christianity and Its Fate," one of Hegel's early, unpublished theological projects. It is by his *Volksreligion* criterion that Abraham is so severely judged, a fact of considerable interest. If Stephen Crites is right in suggesting that the mature Hegel sees secular Protestantism as the *Volksreligion* of modern Europe, then Hegel's early essay would confirm Kierkegaard's view that he ought to repudiate Abraham. See *In the Twilight of Christendom: Hegel vs. Kierkegaard on Faith and History* (Chambersburg: American Academy of Religion, 1972) 41ff. and 55.

[53]*FT*, 57, 59, 62, 74, 77. Cf. *SUD*, 46. For typical Hegelian statements of the state as universal, see *Philosophy of Right* (henceforth *Right*, quoted by paragraph numbers, with A for Addition or *Anmerkung*) 260 and 270A. Cf. *Die Vernunft in die Geschichte* (henceforth *Vernunft*), Johannes Hoffmeister, ed. (Hamburg: Felix Meiner, 1955) 114-15, where the same identification occurs along with a further identification as *das Heilige*. See n. 70 below. This passage, in relation to *Right*, 267, 273, and 276, indicates that Hegel means by "the state" not the narrowly political entity we call the government, but the whole institutionalized life of a people.

of personal conscience, but *Sittlichkeit*, the public life of a people, institutionalized in family, civil society, and the state.[54]

What, then, is the issue that Kierkegaard poses? In the following formulation one must fill in "society" for "universal" and "God" for "absolute" to get the proper meaning. "The paradox of faith is this, that the individual is higher than the universal, that *the individual ... determines his relation to the universal by his relation to the absolute, not his relation to the absolute by his relation to the universal.* The paradox can also be expressed by saying that there is an absolute duty toward God; for in his relationship of duty *the individual as an individual stands related absolutely to the absolute.* . . . If this duty is absolute, the ethical is reduced to a position of relativity. From this it does not follow that the ethical is to be abolished, but it acquires an entirely different expression."[55]

Implicit in these formulae is the charge that Hegel absolutizes the ethical. This would mean that our relation to God is so thoroughly mediated via the social order that faith becomes indistinguishable from socialization, and the individual's relation to God is no longer a personal one. The knight of faith "becomes God's intimate acquaintance . . . and . . . says 'Thou' to God in heaven, whereas even the tragic hero only addresses Him in the third person." Why so? To Kierkegaard the answer is plain. "The tragic hero does not enter into any private relationship with the deity, but for him the ethical is the divine."[56] However, if the social order itself is the divine, then it no longer stands under the judgment of God. This is as alien to Kierkegaard's understanding of the Christian view as the depersonalization of the individual's God relation. "Every individual ought to live in fear and trembling, and so too there is no established order which can do without fear and trembling. . . . And fear and trembling signifies that a God exists—a fact which no man and no established order dare for an instant forget."[57] It is these two themes that Kierkegaard wishes to develop with his claim that for faith the individual is higher than the universal.

---

[54]Both in *FT*, 55 and in *TC*, 88, where he complains about the deification of the established order, Kierkegaard makes specific reference to a central portion of Hegel's analysis of *Moralität*, the discussion in *Right*, 129-40, entitled "Good and Conscience." He finds the limitations Hegel places there on personal conscience to be part of his deification of *Sittlichkeit*.

[55]*FT*, 70. My italics and ellipsis. The second italicized formula is repeated at 55, 62, 81, 111, 113, and 120. The possibility that Abraham might be lost is always associated with the possibility that this principle may be false.

[56]*FT*, 60 and 70. Cf. 87 and 92 and *SUD*, 20-30, where the central category "before God" is explicitly contrasted with the universality of state or nation.

[57]*TC*, 89. See n. 54.

It would be a misunderstanding, however, to think that he means the natural individual, "conceived immediately as physical and psychical."[58] As natural individuals we have our telos in the universal. The aesthetic must sublimate itself in the ethical and the id must learn to subordinate itself to the superego.[59] On this point there is no quarrel between Hegel and Kierkegaard, except that to Kierkegaard Hegel's analysis seems merely two-dimensional in its tendency to remain at the level of interplay between the preethical individual and society.[60] So persistently and energetically does Hegel chisel away at the superiority of the universal to the preethical individual that the finitude of the ethical itself is forgotten.

But while Kierkegaard is eager to relativize the universal as something finite, it would be another misunderstanding to view this as abolishing it or depriving it of all spiritual significance. In its teleological suspension the universal is "not forfeited but . . . preserved."[61] Kierkegaard always rejects the view that the finite is worthless; and Abraham as his knight of faith must be distinguished from the knight of infinite resignation, whether of the stoic or monastic type, because he continues to love the finite. "Abraham, though gray-haired, was young enough to wish to be a father." He is persuaded that "God is concerned about the least things." For him "finiteness tastes . . . just as good as to one who never knew anything higher." He enjoys its blessings "as though the finite life were the surest thing of all," for his is "the heir apparent to the finite."[62]

What distinguishes the knight of faith from the tragic hero, then, is not that one denies while the other affirms spiritual significance for the family and the nation. The issue is the nature of that significance; and Kierkegaard's complaint is that for Hegel the ethical is divine, meaning that "the whole existence of the human race is rounded off completely like a sphere, and the ethical is at once its limit and its content. God becomes an invisible vanishing point, a powerless thought, His power being only in the ethical which is the content of existence."[63] In such a case Abraham would be lost, but so would Hegel. It would be shown that the content of his speculation is substantially different from the content of biblical faith, and it is a central claim

---

[58]*FT*, 54 and 82.

[59]"[I]t is the particular individual who, after he has been subordinated as the particular to the universal, now through the universal becomes the individual who as the particular is superior to the universal" (*FT*, 56).

[60]Though Nietzsche and Heidegger esteem the individual above "the herd" and "the they," Kierkegaard would find their accounts equally flat or two-dimensional.

[61]*FT*, 54. Cf. the passage cited from 70 at n. 55 above.

[62]Ibid., 18, 34, 40, 50.

[63]Ibid., 68.

of his philosophy that the opposite is true. We must ask whether Kierke-gaard's reading of Hegel is fair and accurate.

Hegel's central affirmation about the state, taken in the broad sense as equivalent to *Sittlichkeit* rather than in the narrowly political sense, is that the state is the actuality (*Wirklichkeit, Realisierung*) of reason and freedom. He speaks as an Aristotelian and not as a Platonist when he says this, for far from scorning the real in relation to the ideal, he stands in awe of what he calls *"der ungeheure Überschritt des Innern in das Äussere, der Einbildung der Vernunft in die Realität."* Inwardness becomes actuality as the state, and the universal Idea comes to appearance. But in this instance, at least, *Erscheinung* is itself *das Wesentliche.*[64]

By itself this would not evoke Kierkegaard's complaint, but Hegel consistently interprets the original affirmation to mean that as the actuality of reason and freedom the state is the actuality of the truth whose knowledge, in one of its modes, constitutes religion.[65] This enables him to speak of religion as an abstract essence whose concrete existence is the state.[66]

Hegel's motives are not difficult to fathom. He feels obliged to enter the lists against the "atheism of the ethical world," which finds reason only in nature but not in the world of spirit, and consequently lapses into various forms of antisocial subjectivism.[67] Religion becomes, then, an antisocial principle, for it is "the highest and unholiest contradiction to seek to bind and subject the religious conscience to a secular legislation which for it is something unholy." Hegel finds such a dualism intolerable. "There cannot be two kinds of conscience, one religious and another ethical."[68] This is the sense in which religion is the foundation of the state. For it is in religion that man's conscience "first feels that it lies under an absolute obligation," and consequently "it is in religion we first have any absolute certainty and security as regards the dispositions of men, and duties they owe to the state."[69]

While Hegel is concerned about the dissolution of law and order, Kierkegaard is fearful of their deification. His sensitive ears prick up immediately at the suggestion that the laws of the state are something holy toward which, with the help of religion, we owe an absolute obligation. Things are not looking up for Abraham. Is the boundary between God and the social order being threatened? Anxieties are not lessened by reading that "everything which man

---

[64]*Right,* 270A and *Vernunft,* 114

[65]See the closing sentence of *Right,* 360. Also *Vernunft,* 123; *Religion,* 1:247 = *Werke,* 16:237-38; and *History,* 417 = *Werke,* 12:497.

[66]*Right,* 270A.

[67]For typical examples see the critique of Jacobi in *Faith and Knowledge,* the critique of Fries in the preface to *Right,* and the critique of romantic irony in *Right,* 140A.

[68]PS, 552A.

[69]*Religion,* 1:102-103 = *Werke,* 16:103.

is he owes to the state, in which alone he has his essence. All worth which man has, all spiritual actuality, he has only through the state." Furthermore, the *Bildung* of a nation, which animates the actual state and is the spirit of a people, is *das Heilige*.[70] This is no mere metaphor. Since "the secular is capable of being an embodiment of the true . . . it is now perceived that morality and justice in the state are also divine and commanded by God, and that in point of substance *there is nothing higher or more sacred*." Again, "secular life is the spiritual kingdom in reality [*im Dasein*]," and *"nothing must be considered higher and more sacred than good will towards the state."*[71]

It is possible to sacralize the ethical in this way because we are dealing with the Idea in its actuality. "The Idea in its truth is rationality actualized; and this it is which exists as the state." In other words, "what is divine about the state is the Idea, as it is present on earth."[72] This introduces us to a new aspect of the problem. It is no longer only a question whether the state stands in fear and trembling before God. The Idea is what Hegel understands by perfection. To call the state the Idea's presence on earth is to substitute the state for the Incarnation. Instead of answering the question, Where on earth is God to be found?, by pointing to Jesus of Nazareth, Hegel points to the state.[73] The detailed arguments of *Philosophical Fragments* are designed to show how strenuous an act faith is when it understands Jesus to be the unique and decisive presence of God in human history. For such a faith Abraham is a splendid model, for in his case as well God breaks into human experience in such a way as to call for an intensely personal response for which even the highest *Bildung* is no substitute, and hardly even a preparation.

These statements in which Hegel finds the state to be God's incarnation are most striking. He sometimes speaks in a Spinozistic vein, as when he writes in the preface to the *Philosophy of Right* that "the great thing is to apprehend in the show of the temporal and transient the substance which is immanent and the eternal which is present." This could be taken simply as an affirmation of providence, against which Kierkegaard would have no quarrel except for the implied identification of providence with the state. But when Hegel

---

[70]*Vernunft*, 111, 114-15.

[71]*History*, 422, 442, 449 = *Werke*, 12:502-503, 524, 531. Hegel only appears to qualify the last statement, for he writes, "Or, if religion be looked upon as higher and more sacred, it must involve nothing really alien or opposed to the constitution."

[72]*Right*, 270A and *Vernunft*, 112. On the ethical as the actuality of the truth, see PS, 552A and *History*, 446 = *Werke*, 12:527-28. By the Idea Hegel understands the unity of *Begriff* and *Objectivität*, of the ideal and real, *LL* 213, which explains why it is possible for him to speak of the Idea of the state as "this actual God." *Right*, 258Z.

[73]A more complete account of Hegel's position would require detailed analysis of his interpretation of the Trinity. In the *Phenomenology* and in *Religion* the tendency is to make God the Son, Jesus, primarily of causal importance in relation to God the Spirit, which spirit is actually the human spirit of modern Christendom.

goes beyond Spinozistic categories to speak of God as will and as love, the overtones of incarnation become stronger. "The state is the divine will, in the sense that it is spirit present on earth, unfolding itself to be the actual shape and organization of a world"; and "the love which God is, is in the sphere of actuality conjugal love."[74]

Finally, there are passages where the ethical is identified as the actuality of God himself, without qualification. "It is in the organization of the state that the divine has passed into the sphere of actuality . . . and the secular realm is now justified in and for itself. . . . The true reconciliation whereby the divine realizes itself in the region of actuality is found in the ethical and legal life of the state. This is the true disciplining of secular life."[75] "Man must therefore venerate the state as an earthly deity [*Irdisch-Göttliches*]."[76] "The ethical life [*Sittlichkeit*] is the divine spirit as indwelling in self-consciousness, in its actual presence *as* a nation [*Volk*] and the individuals of the nation."[77]

This last statement belongs to a context that deserves closer scrutiny. At the beginning of the *Anmerkung* to paragraph 552 of the *Encyclopedia* Hegel expresses his agreement with Kant's view that belief in God proceeds from practical reason. This is because the ethical involves a purification of consciousness from subjective opinion and selfish desire. "True religion and true religiosity only issue from the ethical life. Religion is the ethical life as thinking [*die denkende Sittlichkeit*], i.e. becoming aware of the free universality of its concrete essence. Only from the ethical life and by the ethical life is the Idea of God seen to be free spirit. Outside the ethical spirit it is vain to seek for true religion and true religiosity."

At first it seems that Kierkegaard would agree. In his view of the stages of existence the religious presupposes the ethical, for until the subjectivism of the aesthetical attitude has succumbed to the subjectivity that can be called seriousness, the self is in no position to make any sense of talk about God. But Hegel's second and fourth sentences diverge completely from Kierkegaard's way of agreeing with Kant. Religion, as he understands it with the help of Abraham, is not the self-consciousness of the established order, but the

---

[74]*Right*, 270A and *Religion*, 1:251 = *Werke*, 16:240. For Hegel's assimilation of the laws with the divine will and divine commands, see *Religion*, 1:249 = *Werke*, 16:239 and *History*, 423 = *Werke*, 12:503-504.

[75]*Religion*, 3:138 = *Werke*, 17:332.

[76]*Right*, 272Z. In a footnote to his translation Knox reminds us that Kant referred to states as *Erden-Götter* in his essay, *Über den Gemeinspruch: Das mag in der Theorie richtig sein, taught aber night für die Praxis*. The contrast is quite pointed, for while Hegel speaks of veneration, Kant sternly admonishes states for making war, and reminds them of their duty to enter into an international federation bound by international law.

[77]PS, 552A. My italics.

individual's personal relation to God, a relation that relativizes all participation in the life of one's people. In that sense it is only beyond or outside the ethical spirit that true religion and true religiosity are to be found, for in religion the individual finds an allegiance that transcends political, economic, and family bonds.[78]

Hegel directs our attention to these three institutions in the passage before us. He is very fond of contrasting their affirmation by the Reformation to the Roman Catholic monastic vows of chastity, poverty, and obedience.[79] This time that contrast is followed by a reaffirmation of *Sittlichkeit* as the immanence of the divine spirit. "The divine spirit must interpenetrate the entire secular life. . . . But that concrete indwelling is only the aforesaid ethical organizations. It is the morality of marriage as against the sanctity of the celibate order, the morality of economic and industrial action against the sanctity of poverty and its indolence, and the morality of an obedience dedicated to the law of the state as against the sanctity of an obedience from which law and duty are absent and where conscience is enslaved."

This is to say that true religion affirms the family, the economy, and the state as the decisive presence of God on earth and that true religiosity consists in thoroughgoing socialization. Nothing could be further from the faith of which Abraham is father. And yet it is in the very passage before us that two important qualifications of Hegel's position come to light. First, it is not just any state he has in mind, but the modern, secular, Protestant state. This is consistent with his mature philosophy of history, according to which there are three crucial ingredients in the modern world. To begin, Christianity introduced to the world the idea that all are free. Then the Reformation reintroduced this idea with an intensity of inwardness that gave the idea of freedom new depth; and when, in addition, it affirmed marriage, labor, and the state it established the principle that this freedom was not to be something merely inward but was to inform the whole of our life on earth. Finally, the French Revolution took this principle at face value and sought to introduce into worldly life the principle that all are free. If the real is the rational and vice versa, it is because the real *has become* rational and vice versa.[80] It is most

---

[78]Cf. Kierkegaard's quotation of Luke 14:26 about hating family in order to be a disciple of Christ. *FT*, 72.

[79]For other references see *Religion*, 1:250ff. = *Werke*, 16:239ff.; 3:138ff. = 17:332ff.; *History*, 380ff. = *Werke*, 12:457ff.; and 422ff. = 12:502ff. Hegel gave special attention to this theme in an address on the three hundredth anniversary of the Augsburg Confession. See *Berliner Schriften*, Johannes Hoffmeister, ed. (Hamburg: Felix Meiner, 1956) 44ff.

[80]See Franz Rosenzweig, *Hegel und der Staat* (Berlin: Oldenbourg, 1920) 2:79ff. and the discussion by Michael Theunissen in *Die Verwirklichung der Vernunft* (Tübingen: J. C. B. Mohr, 1970) 25ff. For discussion of Hegel's attitude toward the Reformation and the French Revolution, see the essays cited in n. 2 to ch. 4, Ritter's essay, "Hegel

frequently in the context of these themes from the philosophy of history, as in the passage before us, that Hegel speaks of the state as the divine spirit's earthly manifestation.

A second and even more important qualification of Hegel's view is expressed in the statement that "the divine spirit *must* interpenetrate the entire secular life."[81] Hegel regularly speaks with the grammar of imperatives, subjunctives, and optatives. The state or ethical substance *must* or *should* be the earthly manifestation of God, for this is its *task*. It is only *in sich* rational or infinite, based on a principle that it does not fully realize. Though the principle of the modern world was articulated by the Reformation, "We have as yet no reconstruction of the state, of the system of jurisprudence. . . . Spirit does not assume this complete form immediately after the Reformation."[82] Nor has this defect been finally remedied. During the epoch of the French Revolution the world was filled with a jubilation and spiritual enthusiasm "*as if* the reconciliation between the divine and the secular was now first accomplished." But after forty years Hegel saw "the powerlessness of victory" and concluded both his lectures on the philosophy of history and those on the philosophy of religion with a gloomy report on the present scene.[83] We need to consider seriously that even in the preface to the *Philosophy of Right* Hegel describes reason as "the rose in the *cross of the present*."

Will Kierkegaard's anxieties be assuaged by these restrictions on the Hegelian thesis? It is important to keep in mind that his problems are theological and not political. The question is not whether Haym, Carritt, Popper, Hook, et al. are correct in finding an obsequious Prussianism, crypto-Nazism, and various other offenses against modern liberal sensibility in Hegel's view of the state. (Unfortunately Kierkegaard would not have been as upset about these allegations as we might hope.) The question is whether that view, whatever we may think of its specifically political character, is compatible with the kind of faith that knows what fear and trembling before God is all about and that has Abraham as its father.

And Johannes: "You surely cannot expect me to be impressed by the suggestion that it is only to the modern state that Hegel's comments fully apply. That would be to tell me that Abraham and the faith he represents have become obsolete with the passing of time. I, for one, am not able to see the greatness of Abraham as so ephemeral a thing. But even if I could I would

---

and the Reformation" in the volume of his essays cited there, and my own essay, "Hegel and the Reformation," in *History and System: Hegel's Philosophy of History*, Robert L. Perkins, ed. (Albany: SUNY Press, 1984). Ritter gives a sympathetic interpretation of the relation of *Moralität* to *Sittlichkeit* in Hegel, centering on the notion that freedom must be institutionalized.

[81]See the previous paragraph but one. My italics.

[82]*History*, 424 = *Werke*, 12:504.

[83]*History*, 447ff. = *Werke*, 12:529ff. and *Religion*, 3:149ff. = *Werke*, 17:342ff.

never claim that my view was the same in content as the Christian faith. I think it would be more honest to say that I found that faith to be outmoded. (All honor to Lessing.) As it is I can only say that while I admire Abraham's faith more than my limited literary skill can express, I cannot honestly claim to have such a faith, much less to have gone further.

"The second point is more delicate. I have no wish to dispute the view that while people profess allegiance to higher principles than they used to, the world is still far from what it ought to be and the task which those principles set before us remains undone. But from this I conclude that the state, like the individuals who make it up, is both finite and sinful and not even in principle the incarnation of the sacred. While you concede the facts which lead me to this conclusion, you deny their import. For you "philosophy concerns itself only with the glory of the Idea mirroring itself in the history of the world. Philosophy escapes from the weary strife of passions that agitate the surface of society [*Wirklichkeit*] into the calm region of contemplation."[84] But if the Idea mirrors itself in a "weary strife of passions" from which philosophy must make its escape, that *Wirklichkeit,* even if not wholly godforsaken, can scarcely be described as 'the image of the invisible God,' or as 'the effulgence of God's splendor and the stamp of God's very being.'[85] And it remains puzzling to me how philosophy can afford the luxury of a contemplation divorced from repentance and exhortation. But that is an issue we have already discussed. I cannot help but wonder, though—if Abraham had found his social order, imperfect as it was, to be the highest earthly manifestation of the divine, would he ever have been my Abraham?

---

[84]*History,* 457 = *Werke,* 12:540. Cf. *Right,* 258Z and 270Z concerning Hegel's treatment of the obvious defects in the actual vis-à-vis the Idea.

[85]These phrases are from the New Testament accounts of Jesus Christ as the definitive incarnation of God. Col. 1:15 and Heb. 1:3, *NEB.*

Kierkegaard and the Logic of Insanity

6

Feigned madness can be a valuable asset. King David once used it to escape from the Philistines (1 Sam. 21), and a twentieth-century king, Pirandello's Henry IV, used the same trick on a modern philistine culture. Thrown from his horse and struck on the head while on his way to a masquerade party dressed as the Henry of Canossa's chill repentance, he had for twenty years insanely identified himself with the eleventh-century monarch. At least this is what his family, and the court they provided for his humor, thought. As the play opens they are unaware that he has regained his sanity; he has continued to play Henry IV for the last eight of the twenty years, preferring the mad world in which he lived to the sane world to which he would have to return.

The scene in which Henry reveals his sanity to his privy counselors is one that poses some difficult philosophical questions about the logic of insanity.

> Words, words which anyone can interpret in his own manner! That's the way public opinion is formed! And it's a bad look out for a man who finds himself labelled one day with one of these words which everyone repeats: for example "madman" or "imbecile." . . . We're having a joke on those that think I am mad! . . . It's convenient for everybody to insist that certain people are mad, so they can be shut up. Do you know why? Because it's impossible to hear them speak. . . . Do you know what it means to find yourselves face to face with a madman—with one who shakes the foundations of all you have built up in yourselves, your logic, the logic of all your constructions? Madmen, lucky folk! construct without logic, or rather with a logic that flies like a feather. . . . One must see what seems true to these hundred thousand others who are not supposed to be mad! What a magnificent spectacle they afford when they reason! What flowers of logic they scatter![1]

---

[1]Luigi Pirandello, *Henry IV,* in *Naked Masks: Five Plays,* Eric Bentley, ed. (New York: Dutton, 1952).

Who is mad after all? What is the logic, the standard of reason by which a madman is judged mad? Is it sloganistic public opinion,[2] emotive words without fixed meaning? Is the foundation of our intellectual constructions itself a construction? Who is its maker?

What makes this logic or criterion of reasonableness better than the madman's? Is this question decided by majority vote? Is the truth "what seems true to these hundred thousand others who are not supposed to be mad"?

I

Socrates and Søren Kierkegaard would have to be reckoned among the most vigorous and dialectically skillful opponents of the idea that truth is a question of majority opinion. What brings them to mind together in this context is that both philosophers found it necessary to make their point with reference to madness, suggesting that public sanity is far from identical with the wisdom that is philosophy's object. The opening lines of Socrates' second speech in the *Phaedrus* set forth a theme to which Kierkegaard constantly recurs throughout his voluminous writings. "False is the tale that when a lover is at hand favor ought rather to be accorded to one who does not love, on the ground that the former is mad, and the latter sound of mind. That would be right if it were an invariable truth that madness is an evil, but in reality, the greatest blessings come by way of madness, indeed of madness which is heaven-sent."[3] Socrates concludes this opening statement with a reference to "the superiority of heaven-sent madness over man-made sanity."

As a Christian thinker Kierkegaard applies this idea to the problems of faith and reason. When the charge is made that Christianity is sheer madness and utter absurdity, he grants that from a certain point of view it surely is, and then goes on to ask for credentials of that point of view. When it is said that "modern man" finds the incarnation incredible, he acknowledges the sociological fact, but not without pausing to ask who "modern man" may be. He wants to know who is mad after all. Might it possibly be that the madness that is Christian faith is the higher, divine madness that actually possesses the truth that human sanity professes to love?

The roots of this motif in Kierkegaard's works are biblical. For example, his reflection on Abraham in *Fear and Trembling* reveals the standpoint of faith to be in such a radical and uncompromising either/or relationship with all other modes of thought[4] that the one must evidently appear madness to the others, and vice versa. The killing of Isaac (that he did not finally have to do

---

[2]See Marcuse's critique of one-dimensional thinking in *One-Dimensional Man* (Boston: Beacon Press, 1964) esp. chs. 4 and 5, and the suggestion that slogans function hypnotically.

[3]244a, Hackforth translation.

[4]Kierkegaard's favorite terms for non-Christian modes of thought are paganism, the natural man, and the human understanding or reason.

it is irrelevant—he raised the knife) can only be viewed as murder by any secular ethic. Agamemnon, Jephtha, and Brutus may seek to justify their acts by
viewing duty to their people (the state) as higher than duty to their children,[5]
but no such public and possibly higher earthly duty is involved on Mount
Moriah. Only the direct command from the God who is himself the ground of
the ethical could justify this "suspension," or rather, trampling of the ethical.
And such a God is sheer madness to any ethic within the limits of reason alone.
It is equally true that such an ethic is insane *hubris* to a knight of faith like
Abraham, irrespective of any appeals that may be made in the name of Reason, because he is committed to a "wisdom whose secret is foolishness," a
"hope whose form is madness," to a faith that is "what the Greeks called the
divine madness."[6] To appeal to Reason against the command of God would
be, for Abraham and those who follow him in faith, to deny their fundamental
insight that "as against God we are always in the wrong."[7]

The New Testament roots of this divine-madness motif are more frequently
present in Kierkegaard's writings than this Old Testament paradigm. There are
two: the concept of offense and the Pauline statements in the first two chapters of 1 Corinthians. The frequency with which the former appears in the
Gospels, both directly and indirectly,[8] leads Kierkegaard to the conclusion that
Jesus must be the sign of offense if he is to be the object of faith, and that
"these words, 'blessed is he who shall not be offended in me,' belong *essentially* to the preaching about Christ."[9]

The most direct and sustained expression of the second (Pauline) source
is a sermon that Kierkegaard preached in 1844 on 1 Corinthians 2:6-9 with
special emphasis on the "hidden wisdom of God" and the announcement that
"what never originated in the mind of man, God has prepared to those that
love him"[10] But the basic ideas of the larger passage are everywhere present,
even as far back as 1835, three years before his own conversion experience
while he still spoke of Christians as "they." "Philosophy and Christianity cannot, however, be united," he writes. He knows how to confirm this "by de-

---

[5]This is a Hegelian view of the tragic hero. The priority of the state to the family is
developed in his *Philosophy of Right,* and this conflict is given as the paradigm for
tragedy in the *Phenomenology*.

[6]These phrases are found in *FT,* 16-17 and in a journal entry quoted in the trans-
lator's introduction to the older translation. See *Fear and Trembling and The Sickness
unto Death,* Walter Lowrie, trans. (Garden City: Doubleday, 1954) 10. Cf. *FT,* 23.

[7]From the title of the sermon that concludes *Either/Or*. Cf. Psalm 143:2 (NEB): "Bring
not thy servant to trial before thee; against thee no man on earth can be right."

[8]See *TC,* 86ff.

[9]*SUD,* 128.

[10]See the sermon included in *Johannes Climacus or, De Omnibus Dubitandum Est
and A Sermon,* T. H. Croxall, trans. (Stanford: Stanford University Press, 1958) 159-73.

scribing how man as man, outside of Christianity, appears to the Christian. For this purpose it will suffice to recall how Christians regarded the pagans, considered their gods the inventions of devils, their virtues splendid vices . . . and how they themselves declared that their Gospel was to the pagans foolishness and to the Jews a stumbling block."[11] For himself it seemed that "in contrast to paganism—[Christians] are robbed of their manhood by Christianity and are now like the gelding compared to the stallion," and that due to preoccupation with a fixed idea, the Christian sees the world with vision so defective as to deserve the epithet "happy madness."[12]

The same Pauline idea, more sympathetically handled, is what the "acoustic illusion" of the *Philosophical Fragments* is all about. Unbelief is flying the flag of Reason, and in deference to this claim, Christianity presents itself for battle as the Paradox. Reason calls the Paradox absurd folly. The Paradox calls Reason absurd folly. And the point Kierkegaard seems to want to make is not simply that they are absolutely opposed, but that the Paradox has the honor of having started all the name calling. "When the Reason says that it cannot get the Paradox into its head, it was not the Reason that made the discovery but the Paradox, which is so paradoxical as to declare the Reason a blockhead and a dunce. . . . All that the offended consciousness has to say about the Paradox it has learned from the Paradox, though it would like to pose as the discoverer, making use of an acoustic illusion," that is, mistaking its echo of the Paradox for the original statement.[13]

What is the point of vying for the honor of having fired the first shot? It is an attempt to shift the discussion to the real issue. There is no debate between Reason and Paradox about whether there is a great gulf fixed between them. What Reason affirms on this point Paradox affirmed long ago. It now says to Reason, "It is precisely as you say, and the only wonder is that you regard it as an objection."[14] Instead of overworking the obvious, radical difference between the incarnational *Weltanschauung* and all others (paganism, the natural man, human understanding), let's see whether the negative judgment about the former really follows from the reality of this difference.

It is obvious that Kierkegaard is not impressed by the banner of Reason, and this unwillingness to be intimidated by an appeal to Reason reflects a very definite view of what goes by that name. For him, as for Kant, it is *human reason* that is in question, and the adjective is not redundant. Human reason is a doubly contingent point of view regarding the world, before which the Christian paradoxes of revelation and incarnation, sin and atonement need not cower. Let them be madness from its point of view. It remains to be asked

---

[11]*JP*, 3:3247.

[12]Ibid., 1:416.

[13]*PF*, 53.

[14]Ibid., 52.

in all seriousness whether they possess "the superiority of the heaven-sent madness over man-made sanity."

To begin, there is the Kantian point; human reason fails through its essential finitude to be an absolute (perspectiveless) perspective of the world. If, as I have argued in another place,[15] the Kantian distinction between the noumenal and phenomenal worlds is that between the way in which one world appears to God and to us, then the Kantian dualism is fundamental to Kierkegaard's epistemology too. In the *Concluding Unscientific Postscript* the claim to absolute knowledge (philosophy as the divine's knowledge of itself as divine) is treated as one of the most comical of all philosophical howlers, the acme of professional absentmindedness in which, forgetting their names, philosophers identify themselves with the pure I-am-I, the divine self-knowledge. Humor is, of course, the highest mode in which the pseudonym who makes no Christian profession can operate. However, when this limit is no longer present, Kierkegaard is not reluctant to express his own offense at such a project. He calls it blasphemy again and again, thereby giving a theological twist to the Kantian finitism.[16]

Beyond the fact that reason is the broker of finiteness,[17] there is a second and even more important limitation, its openness to temporal conditioning (a Hegelian point turned against Hegel by Kierkegaard and the historical relativists). What goes under the name of reason are the fundamental assumptions of the established order. Reason is ideology, and ideologies are thoroughly historical productions. Because "the established order is the rational," the concept of Christ as madman and the concept of the established order are integrally related; in fact, they are introduced in the same paragraph[18] because one presupposes the other as a foreground requires a background. The clergyman is typical of the numerous representatives of the establishment (wise and prudent men, philosopher, statesman, solid citizen, mocker) who form a self-appointed jury that renders the unanimous verdict that this undeniably unusual fellow who claims to be God is mad. He argues, "But that it is God in his own person that should come is the expectation of no reasonable man. . . . The veritable Expected One will therefore appear totally different; he will come as the most glorious flower and the highest unfolding of the established order. . . . He will recognise the established order as an authority."[19]

Kierkegaard feels he has a right to be suspicious of this "reasonableness" that submits to the *authority* of the established order. That is why he is not

---

[15]See "In Defense of the Thing in Itself," in *Kant-Studien* 59:1 (1968): 118-41.

[16]*TC*, 31-33.

[17]*FT*, 36. Cf. 47.

[18]*TC*, 42, 91.

[19]Ibid., 50, in the context of 45-55.

bashful about calling modern philosophy nothing more than "traditional conceptions," describing Hegelianism as a "new wisdom which I already regard as outdated" (with a reference to the divine-madness theme of the Phaedrus). He even suggests that espousers of Hegel's views on time "must be regarded as mad."[20] When the established order presents itself as "the age" he respects its honesty, even if he cannot refrain from asking whether what the age demands is the same as what it needs. When it presents itself as Reason, he treats this as a confusion that is at best hilarious and at worst intellectually dishonest.

In the light of this account of Reason, it is both possible and necessary to take Kierkegaard's "irrationalism" seriously, precisely where he insists that faith is not merely beyond reason, but against it. It will not do simply to say that human reason is reason as such and in principle free from either or both of the limitations alleged above, for it is ambiguous whether such a view of human reason is not itself a familiar way in which historically conditioned establishments deify themselves. Further, it is possible to hope for a coherent account not only of faith, but also of "faith's capacity to understand"; not only of divine madness, but also of "the logic of insanity" (since this phrase, too, is Kierkegaard's own).[21] It may be that for Kierkegaard, as for Professor Findlay, if mysticism or radical theism is to survive the challenge of more familiar modes of thought that call themselves Reason, "it is not a question of being inconsistent or illogical, but of deciding what form one's consistency or logicality may take."[22] To express "faith's capacity to understand" is to do theology—to employ the language of faith with clarity and precision. To discuss "the logic of insanity" is to articulate the formal structures of this language, to do logic in the familiar, informal sense. Whereas the philosophical logician tries to define "the logical features of ordinary discourse" (Strawson), the theological logician's task is to do the same for the extraordinary language of faith, though for Kierkegaard the boundary between these two tasks is not uncrossable. His work as logician is motivated by two questions. In response to the question whether Christianity can be proved true, he replies with a discussion of the problems of inference and evidence. In response to the question whether it can be proved false, he replies with a discussion of contradiction. We turn now to the first of these discussions.

II

"The man who journeyed from Jerusalem to Jericho and fell among thieves was not so badly off as Christianity; for the orthodox apologetic which had compassion upon it and took care of it treated it quite as badly as the thieves."

---

[20]The first and the third phrases come from *JC*, 127 and 142 n. 17. For the second see *CI*, 13.

[21]*TC*, 81 and 58.

[22]See J. N. Findlay, "The Logic of Mysticism," in *Religious Studies* 2:2 (April 1967): 59.

Less picturesquely, Kierkegaard's point is "that orthodoxy and heterodoxy continue to be enemies who would extirpate one another, in spite of the fact that they want one and the same thing—to make Christianity plausible."[23]

Although Kierkegaard directs his antiapologetic polemic (e.g. "he who first invented the notion of defending Christianity in Christendom is *de facto* Judas No. 2"[24]) primarily at the notion that one can *prove* the reality of God, immortality, the incarnation, and so forth, he does so in such a way as to cut off the usual retreat of the apologist to the humbler claim that he merely seeks to show that Christianity is plausible or probable.[25] Since theological affirmations have to do with concrete existence, it is not surprising that he rejects the "incontrovertible *ergo*" and the "*direct* transition" that are suggested by the assimilation of theological inference to mathematical inference. But it comes as a surprise that he assimilates faith to the mode of belief proper to ordinary historical judgments; for the latter, while never proven in the strictest sense, are sometimes not only plausible, but also in some sense probable.

The difference between the two types of judgment can be understood only in terms of the "will to believe" motif that underlies Kierkegaard's account of their similarity and his rejection of the mathematical model. In the absence of the "incontrovertible ergo," the "direct transition," and the "promptly convinced," which would describe the quasi-mathematical entailment of theological conclusions from incorrigible premises, faith is possible "only by a choice," by "the most frightful act of decision."[26] Similarly, historical judgments possess an objective uncertainty that is negated in belief. The fear of error in such a context can lead to a thoroughgoing skepticism, but the suspension of judgment involved in such a skepticism, since it is a willed *epoche,* can only be overcome by an act of will. The "conclusion" is actually a "resolution." It involves a *decision* (a) to abandon what Hegel was fond of calling the I-won't-go-into-the-water-until-I'm-sure-I-can-swim attitude and (b) to accept a particular set of suggesting reasons as confirming reasons for the assertion that is made. The question about this *leap* that somehow bridges the gap between the *data* that are the initial premises of the inferences involved and the *conclusions* that they do not entail is the question of *warrants* in a voluntaristic context.

It is with Lessing's help that Kierkegaard formulates the question. He always sees the nonentailment just referred to as the "ugly, broad ditch" that, Lessing says, "I cannot get across, however often and however earnestly I have

---

[23]*OAR,* 60.

[24]*SUD,* 87.

[25]*PF,* 52, 94ff.; *OAR,* 59-60; *JP,* 1:7; *CUP,* 189.

[26]*TC,* 98-100; *PF,* 79ff.

tried to make the leap."[27] Yet he realizes that the premises of the traditional apologetic, while not entailing the conclusions drawn from them, have stood in some relation to those conclusions. They have at least served as occasions. The question of warrants becomes the question of how this is possible. A transcendental deduction is required.

For Lessing the theological conclusions were "necessary truths of reason," this being understood in a Spinozistic-Leibnizian way. It is clear that empirical (contingent) propositions of any sort can stand in no evidential relation to such truths. So the warrant by which the data become an occasion is not a rule of inference that establishes such an evidential relationship. What then could it be? The data, as empirical and contingent, can neither support nor provide content for the conclusion that, on the contrary, stands as the criterion for the possibility and meaning of the former. In this particular case Lessing's Spinozistic view of God, taken as a necessary truth of reason, sets limits to the meaning of the historical life of Jesus and excludes the possibility of his life being an incarnation. The historical data can only serve as the occasion for recollection of the necessary truths that do not depend upon it, just as Socrates' questions and diagrams evoked geometrical truth from the slave boy. This assimilation of Lessing's view of theological propositions as necessary truths of reason with the Socratic affirmations that the Truth is within us and that knowledge is recollection expresses a distinctive answer to the question of warrants. The warrant and the conclusion are the same. They differ only as potentially or actually recollected. Lessing's formula is this:

Data as occasion + the Truth within = knowledge as recollected Truth.

There is really no inference here, or, if you prefer, only a question begging one, since the conclusion is one of the premises.

Kierkegaard cannot accept this account. His thought moves toward bridging the gap in question by a leap that is more an act of will than of intellect, a resolution rather than a recollection. This voluntarism is a corollary of his view of reason as both finite and temporally conditioned. It leads him to see "necessary truths of reason" as necessary only within the context of an established order that defines a particular brand of reason, that is, only subsequent to the adoption (choice) of meaning postulates that are themselves contingent. Kierkegaard has no patience for attempts to cover this up by talking about Reason. The dogmatism that he complains against is not that of affirming something and then, consistently, rejecting the alternatives as false. Anyone who believes anything does this. His complaint is directed against the attempt to provide absolute guarantees that preclude even the possibility of being wrong. Lessing's a priori combined with his theory of it as a necessary truth of reason make it impossible for him to recognize an incarnation should it occur, since he knows in advance that it is not possible. Kierke-

---

[27]*Lessing's Theological Writings,* Henry Chadwick, trans. (Stanford: Stanford University Press, 1957) 55.

gaard, on the other hand, agrees with William James that "a rule of thinking which would absolutely prevent me from acknowledging certain kinds of truth if those kinds of truth were really there, would be an irrational rule." And if James is inclined to describe such an approach as "an insane logic," Kierkegaard will agree and suggest that his logic of insanity is, among other things, a passionate protest against every insane logic. If James is inclined to view the absolute veto that such a logic issues as "the queerest idol ever manufactured in the philosophic cave," Kierkegaard also sees in the deification of the established order that underlies such a claim to absoluteness "the constant rebellion, the permanent revolt against God."[28]

So we are asked to consider the other possibility—that human reason is doubly defective, that the Truth is not within us, even that we not only lack it but stand in a polemical relation to it. (It is this last point that essentially distinguishes theological judgments from ordinary historical judgments.) The data, of course, still do not provide premises that entail the conclusion of faith, and it is one thing to be an eyewitness to the life of Jesus, quite another to be an eyewitness disciple. The historical data serve only as signs that point noncoercively in the direction of faith, signs whose true meaning can be missed through either misinterpretation or the failure to recognize even their function as signs. Since, on the present assumption, the Truth is not within us, and the function of these signs therefore cannot be to remind us of what we in some sense already know, it becomes a pressing question how they can ever be correctly interpreted, how they can ever function as the occasion for faith. The condition for interpreting them correctly must be given to us, who, if the Truth is not within us, do not have it; for to say that the Truth is within us is simply to say that we are able to recognize it as such when confronted with it. We need therefore, not only a Teacher who can confront us with the Truth, but also one who can implant within us the condition for recognizing it as such. This fundamental remaking is nothing short of an act of re-creation, and the one who performs it is not just a Teacher but a Savior.

Thus instead of Lessing's formula we have a very different formula:

Data as occasion + the giving of the condition = faith as miracle.

That the end product is called both faith and miracle is appropriate since Kierkegaard emphasizes both the divine activity, the giving of the Truth and condition, and the human response, the act of obedience and trust that is a leap of faith, though he does not present a theory of how they are related.

The warrant here is very different from Lessing's. It is not the Truth within us but rather Truth given to us by the divine grace that grants the condition for recognizing it. Nothing here is introduced to free the situation from the objective uncertainty natural to the doubly limited human understanding. Neither sensible certainty nor rational self-evidence enters the scene to pro-

---

[28]*Essays on Faith and Morals* (New York: World Publishing Company, 1962) 56-61; and *TC*, 89.

vide guarantees against the possibility of being mistaken or an absolute veto against alternatives. There is no easy retreat to probability or plausibility, for apart from the warrant that the condition provides, the data do not stand in *any* evidential relation to the conclusion of faith. The question is not so much whether there is enough evidence, but whether there is any at all. If there is any, there is more than enough.

This discussion with Lessing about the incarnation is illuminated by a comparison with comments about attempts to prove the existence of God. Would we prove the existence of God from the works of God, that is, those which only God could perform?

> Just so, but where then are the works of the God? The works from which I would deduce his existence are not directly and immediately given. The wisdom in nature, the goodness, the wisdom in the governance of the world—are all these manifest, perhaps, upon the very face of things? . . . From what works then do I propose to derive the proof? From the works as apprehended through an ideal interpretation, i.e. such as they do not immediately reveal themselves. But in that case it is not from the works that I make the proof; I merely develop the ideality I have presupposed. . . . In beginning my proof I presuppose the ideal interpretation, and also that I will be successful in carrying it through; but what else is this but to presuppose that God exists, so that I really begin by virtue of confidence in him?[29]

And so the conclusion of the argument emerges from it only by the leap in which one adopts (chooses) the interpretation (warrant) by which the works are seen to be the works of God. The question-begging character of the process is evident. Kierkegaard's logic of the insanity of faith, far from denying this circular character of theological proofs, calls our attention to it in opposition to the insane logic of both the orthodox apologetics and their freethinking opponents. It directs our attention to the necessity of choice and the inescapability of the leap. It reminds us that theological affirmation is grounded in presuppositions that are chosen, not proven.

III

Kierkegaard refers to Sextus Empiricus in his analysis of the question-begging character of theological proofs. It will be evident that his analysis of the proof for the existence of God from the works of God has the same formal structure as Sextus's critique of the syllogism, according to which the major premise can be known to be true only if the conclusion is also known to be true. Or, as Mill restated the same point, the major premise is the warrant that validates the inference from the minor premise to the conclusion, which therefore emerges from the proof as its conclusion only in virtue of the leap by which the major premise is adopted.

This raises the question whether Kierkegaard's position is another version of the nominalistic skepticism that runs from Sextus through Hume and Mill

---

[29]*PF*, 42.

to many contemporary thinkers. Is Kierkegaard an empiricist in this sense of the word?

I believe not. To say this is not to underestimate the importance of his study of the ancient skeptics, but rather to recognize that he is always pushing beyond them, even if he finds it necessary to pass through their territory. His discussion of the skeptical epoche with regard to ordinary empirical (historical) judgments was directed at contrasting a will to believe with the skeptical will to suspend judgment, a fear of missed truth with the skeptical fear of error. The Jamesian character of this action reminds us that movement in Mill's direction is not the only alternative for one who is enough of an empiricist to deny the existence of "coercive evidence" for questions of fact.

Kierkegaard's argument as a whole fits more completely into a tradition other than the Sextus-Hume-Mill line. This is the voluntarist tradition where James corresponds to Mill, Fichte to Hume, and Augustine to Sextus Empiricus. Sufficient reference to James's position has already been made. Fichte's position is best expressed in his *Erste Einleitung in die Wissenschaftslehre*. After distinguishing idealism from dogmatism, he asks which is correct. "Reason provides no ground for a decision. . . . It is therefore a matter of choice [*durch Willkür*], and since even the resolution of free choice [*der Entschluss der Willkür*] needs some ground, it is determined through inclination and interest. . . . Thus what kind of philosophy one chooses depends on what kind of man he is."[30] It would be linguistically permissible to introduce the notion of arbitrariness in rendering the double reference to *Willkür,* but in the context it would obliterate one of the important aspects of Fichte's position. The decision may be arbitrary with respect to reason considered as the theoretical comprehension of the conditioned, since the question is about the unconditioned; but it is not entirely arbitrary. Fichte renders the question of decision an ethical question by making it a matter of inclination and interest. James had done this in a weak sense by speaking of the *right* to believe (under certain conditions) without coercive evidence, but Fichte seems to suggest that one has a *duty* in this matter. That would certainly be the implication in the Kantian context of introducing inclination and interest; how these affect our decisions and which inclinations and interests prevail is *the* ethical question. That Fichte is still a Kantian in this regard is clear because he continues, in the passage just cited, to list a number of vices that would automatically lead to the adoption of dogmatism rather than idealism.

That the question of faith is finally an ethical question is one of Kierkegaard's central themes, and thus he understands faith dialectically in terms of its opposites, which are not doubt, but rather despair, disobedience, offense, and resignation, all of which turn out to be forms of sin. Referring to *Philosophical Fragments* and *The Sickness unto Death,* Kierkegaard writes:

---

[30]*Science of Knowledge with the First and Second Introductions,* Peter Heath and John Lachs, trans. (New York: Meredith Corporation, 1970) 14-16.

It has been shown that in recent philosophy confusion has been wrought by talk-ing about doubt where one ought to speak of despair. . . . Despair, on the other hand, at once indicates the right direction by bringing the relationship under the concept of personality (the individual) or under the rubric of ethics. But just as people have talked confusingly about "doubt" instead of talking about "despair," so also it has been customary to employ the category "doubt" where one ought to speak of "offence."

Because modern philosophy thus fails to see faith, through despair and of-fense as its opposites, as an "ethical," "religious," and "existential" question, it invites us "to be conceited because they doubt or have doubted."[31]

Similarly, in *On Authority and Revelation*, faith is viewed as a response to revelation, a relation of person to person. In terms of the authority inherent in divine revelation, the question of faith becomes an ethicoreligious ques-tion of obedience to God. "The question is quite simple: Will you obey? or will you not obey? Will you bow in faith before his divine authority? Or will you be offended? Or will you perhaps take no side? Beware! this also is of-fence."[32]

This ethicizing of the question of faith marks a distinctive difference be-tween Kierkegaard, along with Fichte and James, and the tradition of Sextus, Hume, and Mill. Nevertheless, it could be argued that since the possibility of such a move presupposes a skepticism about objective and coercive meth-ods for settling ultimate questions, the former group is able to "go beyond" the latter only by presupposing the nominalistic skepticism with which the latter were content to rest.

But not every skepticism is nominalistic. One of Kierkegaard's strongest statements about the personal and ethical dimensions of faith is a journal en-try: "Therefore the *obedience* [his italics] of faith (i.e. Romans 1:5) is the ap-ostolic expression; then faith is oriented toward will, personality, not toward intellectuality."[33] This is part of a complaint against Augustine for reducing the concept of faith to assent, thereby assimilating it to the Platonic problem of opinion and knowledge, and robbing it of its existential dimensions. While there are undeniable grounds for this complaint in Augustine's work, Kier-kegaard's logic of insanity is in an important sense Augustinian, for it also operates in the mode of faith seeking understanding. This affinity is relevant to the question at hand.

No one would be tempted to call Augustine a nominalist. Yet he says the same things about proving the existence of God that Kierkegaard says. His famous "proof" from the reality of Truth, as it appears in *De Liberum Arbi-trium*, is entirely within the framework of *credo ut intelligam*. It is given by a believer to a believer, both of whom confess their belief in God's existence

---

[31]*TC*, 83n.

[32]*OAR*, 26. Cf. liv and 116-17.

[33]*JP*, 1:180.

before and during, as well as after the proof. They may believe that everyone should recognize the force of the proof, but they do not treat it as an objective and coercive weapon. Instead they talk as if the force of the proof depended upon their previous faith. To repeat, it is not belief but understanding that they seek. The belief rests upon an acceptance of the biblical revelation as authoritative. Reason, as it seeks to "prove" what faith believes, recognizes that it is "mutable, now struggling to arrive at truth, now ceasing to struggle, sometimes reaching it and sometimes not. . . . Reason discerns that it is inferior." Therefore the entire investigation of the treatise is undertaken, "depending on [God] and praying for his help" and in the confidence that "we shall find him when he himself shows us." If there is an appeal to "the truth within which teaches us," the power to find the answer through this "highest teacher of all" is something Augustine hopes God will give to Evodius.[34]

Talk like this would surely sound strange on the lips of Socrates or Lessing. We are reminded that the Augustinian doctrine of illumination is not simply a Platonic way of talking about knowledge, but a Platonic way of expressing a Christian epistemology. For the truth within, the highest teacher is Christ, who in his noetic function (John 1:9) is said to dwell in everyone, but whose noetic efficacy is dependent upon the moral condition of the individual and thus ultimately upon regeneration because the limitations of reason are primarily due to sin. Vice, not finitude, bars the door of truth.

In this context it is clear that the priority of faith to reason and the consequent question-begging character of proofs, if taken to be something other than faith seeking understanding, do not rest upon a nominalist account of the finitude of human reason, but upon a theological account of its limits. In the light of what Kierkegaard says about our polemical relation in sin to the truth and about the dichotomy of faith and sin, it is clear that his theory of the limits of human understanding is a theological theory like Augustine's. Not just Kantian finitude and Hegelian historicity, both of which could be built upon nominalist foundations but, above all, Augustinian sinfulness stands between human reason and the truth.

Joined to Kierkegaard's mention of Sextus Empiricus is a reference to Protagoras; this provides the opportunity for expanding our investigation of Kierkegaard's relation to empiricism, in particular to a couple of closely related Protagorean elements of twentieth-century empiricism: the conventionalist theory of necessary truth and the noncognitivist account of religious language. The theory of the *a priori* that Kierkegaard sets against Lessing's appears to have at least some affinities with these two elements of logical empiricism. It was, for example, quite natural to introduce the Carnapian notion of meaning postulates when speaking of Kierkegaard's theory of war-

---

[34]*On the Free Choice of the Will,* Anna S. Benjamin and L. H. Hackstaff, trans. (Indianapolis: Bobbs-Merrill, 1964) 38, 49, 13, and 39.

rants.[35] In opposition to Lessing's treatment of necessary truths of reason, Kierkegaard, like Carnap, is willing to grant only a hypothetical and not a categorical necessity, the condition being the adoption of necessary presuppositions, whether these be called meaning postulates, ideal interpretations, or warrants. Both give theories of necessary truth *for me* or *for us*, —that is, for those who adopt the suitable framework of postulates—and both describe the adoption as a matter of choice.[36]

However, there is a crucial difference (other than the obvious fact that Kierkegaard is not giving a theory that explicitly applies to all necessary or a priori truth). When it comes to comparing alternative frameworks or postulate sets and deciding which one to adopt, Carnap leaves the question at the level of expediency, adopting a kind of pragmatic noncognitivism. Concerning the choice between the postulates of realism and those of phenomenalism, he writes, "If someone decides to accept the thing language, there is no objection against saying that he has accepted the world of things. But this must not be interpreted as if it meant his acceptance of a *belief* [his italics] in the reality of the thing world; there is no such belief or assertion or assumption, because it is not a theoretical question. To accept the thing world means nothing more than to accept a certain form of language." This means, among other things, to accept a certain set of inferences.[37]

Hare introduced the well-known concept of "bliks" for expressing this sort of noncognitivism and its application to theological statements. He suggested that certain fundamental theological statements, including "God exists," are neither true nor false, but are bliks. Like our "belief" in the uniformity of nature based on Hume's analysis and our "belief" in the reality of the external world based on Carnap's, such statements are the rules of inference or interpretation by which the truth or falsity of other statements is determined, and as such they are not true or false themselves. They may be sane or insane, and this introduction of the notion of insanity into the analysis of warrants, inference, and the a priori brings us right back to Kierkegaard. What is the relation of his analysis of Christian faith as divine madness to Hare's analysis of the insane blik of a poor fellow who was convinced that all the Oxford dons wanted to murder him?

Given the blik in question, our lunatic will accept no behavior of the dons as evidence that they are really friendly toward him. What appear to be signs

---

[35]The relation between a theory of the analytic and a theory of inference is a very direct one. Thus meaning postulates can be described as rules that relate predicates in a language so that certain entailments take place, and entailment can in turn be defined in terms of analyticity ('P' entails 'Q' = df 'if P then Q' is analytic). Carnap proceeds in the first way, Strawson in the second.

[36]For Carnap's statements, see *Meaning and Necessity: A Study in Semantics and Modal Logic* (Chicago: University of Chicago Press, 1956) 207, 225.

[37]Ibid., 207.

of friendship he sees only as their "diabolical cunning." Of course, he may be right. He may be the victim of a diabolical conspiracy, and he may be in a better position to see through its camouflage than anyone else around. Nevertheless, he is judged insane, and the reason is quite clear: his blik differs from ours. This rephrases Kierkegaard's point that we consider those whose warrants differ radically from our own to be mad.

A further similarity is that Hare's lunatic, like Kierkegaard's believer, is no friend of Lessing and his insane logic. For while the lunatic will not accept anything presented to him as counting decisively against his conclusions, he does not have the courage (insanity) to say that nothing could ever come to count against it or even persuade him to abandon it.

There remains, however, one important difference. Kierkegaard does not share Hare's noncognitive interpretation of the bliks in question. While he denies that human understanding can have an objective certainty about the truth value of conflicting theological bliks, he never moves to make the question of choice a question of usefulness, a consequence that Carnap consistently draws from the noncognitive analysis. Kierkegaard affirms that reality is a system for God.[38] This means that there is a cognitive point of view that defines the truth values of conflicting bliks. God knows whether the Oxford dons are really in conspiracy against our poor friend. Although Kierkegaard insists that he cannot objectively settle the dispute between those whose theological a prioris differ radically, he never suggests that the issue between them is not one of truth or falsity. Only on the assumption that it is an issue of truth or falsity can the questions of our eternal happiness have the intensity of pathos that they achieve in Kierkegaard's writing and experience. The ease with which he speaks of God and immortality as possibilities to be taken seriously suggests that however problematic he may find theological truth claims, when it comes to questions of meaning, his affinities lie with the eschatological verificationists rather than with the noncognitivists.

IV

It is time to turn from questions about inference and evidence to the theory of judgment, for the serious objection remains that the whole preceding discussion is pointless inasmuch as Kierkegaard holds that the essential affirmations of Christian faith are self-contradictory, paradoxical, and absurd. Perhaps an open mind toward theism requires one to consider seriously the idea that the content of faith is a kind of madness, possibly divine, vis-à-vis ordinary human thinking. However, when the reason "against" which faith believes is not "what the age demands," but the simple requirement that one not simultaneously affirm "p" and "not-p," isn't that too much to swallow?

Granted, but is it so clear that this is what we are asked to swallow? The central contradiction (paradox, absurdity) of Christian faith is the incarna-

---

[38]*CUP*, 107.

tion, according to Kierkegaard, and the question is whether he holds its affirmation to be the simultaneous affirmation of some proposition and its denial. To begin with, the terms "absurd" and "paradox" do not suggest this. For example, "Faith therefore hopes for this life, but, be it noted, by virtue of the absurd, not by virtue of human understanding. . . . Faith is therefore what the Greeks called the divine madness."[39] As before, the contrast is not between formal consistency and formal inconsistency, but between the human understanding and the divine madness. This contrast has to do, not with logical consistency, but with real possibility. In *Fear and Trembling* the knight of faith gives up the beloved, saying, "I believe nevertheless that I shall get her, in virtue, that is, of the absurd, in virtue of the fact that with God all things are possible." The author's comment on this is that "at the moment when the knight made the act of resignation, he was convinced, humanly speaking, of the impossibility. This was the result reached by the understanding."[40] To believe by virtue of the absurd or, what is the same thing, to believe the absurd,[41] is to consider possible what is impossible, humanly speaking, because God has been left out of the account. "God can appear to man only in the miracle. . . . To see God or to see the miracle is by virtue of the absurd, for understanding must step aside. . . . But Christianity, which always turns the concepts of the natural man upside down and gets the opposite meaning out of them, relates πίστις to the improbable. This concept of improbability, the absurd, ought, then, to be developed."[42] As the sign of the miraculous and the humanly improbable, the category of the absurd is "the negative criterion of the divine or of relationship to the divine . . . of that which is higher than human understanding and knowledge."[43]

The situation is similar with the notion of paradox, which Kierkegaard treats as synonymous with the notion of the absurd. In the *Philosophical Fragments* it is presented in a strikingly Kantian context as equivalent to the unconditioned, which, so far from being self-contradictory, serves to reveal the internal contradictions in ordinary human thinking. In the *Postscript* paradoxical religiousness is that which must be believed "against the understanding," which in that context clearly means against the common human understanding and its "immanence thinking," not against formal consistency. Or again, in *On Authority and Revelation,* the paradox is found because the apostle, who is merely an individual, is superior to the established order (the universal). As in *Fear and Trembling* where a similarly paradoxical inversion of the normal relation involved the ethical rather than the epistemic, the paradoxi-

---

[39] *JP,* 1:5.

[40] *FT,* 46-47.

[41] *JP,* 1:11.

[42] Ibid., 1:7.

[43] Ibid., 1:10-11.

cal element is simply the tension between God's activity and the way things would be if he were not involved. The unique position of the apostle "can be explained only by the fact that it is God who makes use of him."[44] Nowhere is there a hint that the paradoxical is the formally self-contradictory.

But Kierkegaard is not content to describe Christian faith and its content as absurd and paradoxical. He constantly calls it self-contradictory. Is this simply another forceful way of expressing the divine madness theme, or is he saying that faith is no respecter of the law of contradiction? We dare not assume that Kierkegaard, speaking in a Hegelian context, must mean by "contradiction" what we mean by it in the context of the propositional calculus, since he may well have learned from Hegel how to use the term in a variety of nonformal senses to refer to otherness, conflict, tension, and so forth; but neither can we assume without evidence that he means the same by "contradictory" as "absurd" and "paradoxical." We must look at the way he uses the term to see whether it stays within the limits of what he elsewhere says about the logic of insanity, or whether it adds a new and more radical dimension. Such a look provides ample evidence that the former alternative is the case.

One of the strongest indications of this is the way in which the madness motif and the notion of the self-contradictory are used interchangeably in *Training in Christianity*.[45] Precisely where faith is described as madness one can expect to find it described as self-contradictory; and often this latter characteristic, like the former, is explicitly relative to the established order and human understanding. It is not only the incarnation that is described in this way, and the other definitions are very instructive. For example, "Humanly speaking, this is indeed the craziest contradiction, that he who literally 'has nowhere to lay his head,' that a person of whom (humanly) it was appropriately said, 'Behold the man!' that he says, 'Come hither to me, all ye that suffer—I will help!' "[46] Other "contradictions" are that a compassion so sublime, so divine as to be concerned for the sufferer alone and to make itself literally one with the most miserable in order to help them should become actual in daily life; that the Inviter of the poor, sick, and suffering really thought that sin is man's ruin and therefore offered them forgiveness; that the most frightful act of decision that was necessary for the contemporaries of Christ is no longer needed, since the truth of Christianity is now proved; that God, in becoming human, should become a lowly, poor, impotent, and suffering man; that the remedy offered by the Inviter appears worse than the disease; that the needy who respond to the Inviter's promise of help should thereby meet with persecution, and that those who oppose those who carry this word of invitation to the needy should think they are performing a divine service. It is in this con-

---

[44]*OAR*, 192-93.

[45]*TC*, 42, 62-66, 82, 100, 105, 112-13, 116-18, 121, 129.

[46]Ibid., 42.

text that the incarnation and the Christian message as a whole are said to be contradictions.[47]

The Journals of 1850 indicate beyond question that Kierkegaard personally affirmed the doctrine of the absurd and the paradoxical that appears in the works of his pseudonyms, Johannes de Silentio and Johannes Climacus. A similar unity of doctrine concerning the issue of contradiction is to be found between Kierkegaard's own views as expressed in *Training in Christianity*[48] and those of his pseudonym in the *Postscript*. There Johannes Climacus discovers the essence of the comical to be the contradictory. Thus he finds it comical (because it is contradictory) to think that walking on one's knees is a way of pleasing God; to do wrong knowingly, and then seek to erase the action by calling it unjustified; to swear, as Hamlet did, by the fire-tongs; to stake one's life on the value of a book's binding; or to offer to give one's life for one's country—for ten dollars.[49] In these and endless other examples of the comical that Kierkegaard gives, the contradiction that is their essence is not the affirmation of "p" and "not-p" together. Instead it lies in the conjunction of elements that are ordinarily incongruous.

Returning to the religious, Kierkegaard sees the same incongruity in the idea that an eternal happiness is based upon something historical; that, consequently, an infinite passion, faith, is directed toward that of which only imperfect knowledge (approximation) is possible; and that one who is already created becomes a Christian by the miracle of creation, by becoming a new creature. Therefore these too are "contradictions." Finally, there is the further dialectical contradiction that the historical fact in question is not an ordinary historical fact, but an incarnation. It "is constituted by that which only against its nature can become historical, hence by virtue of the absurd."[50]

As in *Training in Christianity,* the affirmation of the incarnation as a contradiction is embedded in a context that forbids us to take this in a formal sense. The only possible ground for another understanding of Kierkegaard here is that what becomes historical in the incarnation does so "against its nature." But when the iron axe head floated for Elisha and when Lazarus rose from the dead at the command of Jesus, they certainly did so against their nature, though I do not formally contradict myself if I affirm these events, nor utter a tautology if I deny them. The impossibility of things behaving contrary to their nature is not a logical impossibility. Kierkegaard confirms this understanding of his statement by reintroducing the category of the absurd, the sign of the miraculous.

---

[47]These "contradictions" are found in the passages listed in n. 45 above.

[48]Following Lowrie's argument, I take *Training in Christianity* to be a non-pseudonymous work.

[49]*CUP,* 413n and 458ff.

[50]Ibid., 508-12.

So Kierkegaard leaves us with "the most frightful act of decision". The choice is between unbelief, which finds sheer madness in the affirmations of faith, and belief, which sees in that madness a divine wisdom. If Kierkegaard's analysis of inference and evidence robs belief of the security of objective proof, his analysis of the absurd, the paradoxical, and the contradictory robs unbelief of the security of an easy dismissal on the grounds that the content refutes itself. It is not the task of his logic of insanity to settle the substantial issue, though his personal stance is never in question.

At the end of his life, Ibsen's Brand hears a voice from heaven declare that man's redemption is by God's love. This message stands in stark opposition not only to the careless indifference of the common people, but also to his own rigoristic moralism. He learns this truth in the Ice Church on the peaks high above the scene in which his earlier life and those of his worldly opponents transpired. It is a genuinely Kierkegaardian inspiration that provides for Brand as his Beatrice in the realm of the Ice Church, the mad gypsy girl, Gerd.

Inwardness and Ideology Critique in Kierkegaard's *Fragments* and *Postscript*

7

Introduction

It is the thesis of this essay that in the person of Johannes Climacus Kierkegaard combined a Lutheran understanding of the noetic effects of sin with the essential insights of the sociology of knowledge to produce a theologically grounded critique of the society in which he lived. Since the kind of social criticism that results is referred to today as ideology critique, we can apply that term, anachronistically but informatively, to the writings of Johannes; and since those writings are decisively oriented, not to speculation but to the edification that seeks to evoke the inwardness that Johannes identifies as ethicoreligious subjectivity, we can speak here of the marriage of inwardness and ideology critique.

This thesis is revisionist in at least three senses. If it can be sustained, substantive revisions will be required in three widely held views. The first view is that Kierkegaard is an irrationalist. The second is that by virtue of its individualism his thought is essentially apolitical (whatever his personal views may have been). The third is that ideology critique is an intellectual enterprise that concerns itself with religion only from the perspective of hostile unbelief.

A further word may be in order about this last viewpoint. Ideology critique has its roots in Marxist tradition. It practices what has come to be called the hermeneutics of suspicion. Many writers have noted the affinity of Nietzsche and Freud to Marx and to each other on this score, and Paul Ricoeur has referred to these three as the "masters" who "dominate the school of suspicion."[1] In spite of obvious and perhaps irreconcilable differences among these three, it is helpful to note the dual affinities among them with reference to

---

[1]Paul Ricoeur, *Freud and Philosophy: An Essay on Interpretation,* Denis Savage, trans. (New Haven: Yale University Press, 1970) 32.

hermeneutics and suspicion. But since these three undisputed masters of suspicion are also outspoken atheists, it is all too easy to link their method with their militant unbelief. If it should turn out that as passionate a Christian as Kierkegaard is also a master in the school of suspicion, revisions will be necessary to evaluate the religious significance of both the method and specific applications of it by Marx, Nietzsche, and Freud.

For these three secular masters of suspicion the illusions that must be unmasked are those of self-interest masquerading as duty and virtue, and egoism pretending to the world and to itself that it is altruism. Nietzsche's example of the spirit of resentment giving rise to a demand for revenge but posing as the love of justice is a kind of paradigm. But sin is more than selfishness vis-à-vis my neighbor. It is also the failure to love God with all my heart. Human self-assertion that cannot be openly acknowledged and therefore gives rise to self-deception now includes the will to autonomy from God alongside the will to dominance over my neighbor. Inevitably its introduction into the story adds a whole new dimension to the art of suspicion.

This inward arrogance of the soul is, of course, nothing new to long traditions of both Western and Eastern spirituality. What is distinctive about Kierkegaard's project is the union of the suspicion of inward spirituality with social critique. By integrating the concept of sin into ideology critique he does two things at once. He pushes ideology critique beyond the moral dichotomy of egoism and altruism to the religious dichotomy of obedience and rebellion, faith and offense; and he gives a social, this-worldly dimension to a long tradition of inward, spiritual self-examination. It is difficult to imagine a more explosive marriage than this one between the spirit of Thomas à Kempis and that of Karl Marx. Kierkegaard himself was neither a St. Francis nor a Mohandas Gandhi, nor even a Socrates; but through Johannes Climacus he sets these men before us as subversive saints who are the models of true faith.

Luther on Sin and Reason

Since we are looking at a Lutheran thinker in a Lutheran setting, we should begin with the Lutheran background to Johannes Climacus's critique of reason as ideology. The point is not one of sources but of substance.[2] My claim is that Kierkegaard's use of sin as an epistemological category echoes Luther's view of the noetic effects of the fall.[3] Climacus himself points us in this

---

[2]Kierkegaard's intensive reading of Luther began about the time that Johannes Climacus disappeared from the scene, and even then he devoted himself primarily to the sermons while I will be working from the commentaries. For his reading of Luther, see *JP*, 3, *pages* 802-804, with bibliography, and *PF*, 226, in the older translation by David Swenson and Howard Hong (Princeton: Princeton University Press, 1962).

[3]In both the *Fragments* and the *Postscript* Johannes Climacus is careful not to identify with either the Socratic-Hegelian perspective of immanence or the Christian perspective of transcendence, but only to delineate their fundamental difference. See,

direction in the *Fragments* by noting Luther's view of "Reason [as] a block-head and a dunce," and in the *Postscript* by suggesting the analogy, Luther : Rome = Kierkegaard : Hegel.[4] Thulstrup tells us that Luther did not use the terms "blockhead" and "dunce" to describe reason, but he does evoke the image of Hydra in speaking of "the heads of the beast called reason, which is the fountainhead of all evils," and he calls reason "God's bitterest and most harmful enemy . . . the greatest and most invincible enemy of God, because it despises God and denies His wisdom, justice, power, truthfulness, mercy, majesty, and divinity."[5]

As if the forces outside of us were not powerful enough in their opposition to the gospel of grace, "In addition, we are opposed by half of our very selves, namely, by reason and all its powers." Since this is what we find within us, "The true knowledge of these doctrines does not depend upon the intelligence and wisdom of human reason, nor is it born, so to speak, in our home or in our hearts. But it is revealed and given from heaven."[6] This is the direct antithesis of the Socratic-Hegelian thesis that the Truth is within us.

As the enemy within us, an ally of the law in opposition to the gospel of grace, reason is often identified by Luther with the flesh in its opposition to the Spirit.[7] This identification makes it clear that Luther has no Platonic, gnostic, dualistic view of the flesh, as if it represented the lowest in us against the highest, the bodily and animal side of our nature against the mental and divine side. His is instead a Pauline view, according to which the flesh includes even the highest in us whenever it declares its autonomy in relation to God's sovereignty.[8] Thus reason as an expression of the flesh is human thought un-

---

for example, *CUP*, 330 and 338. It is quite clear that the position he develops as an alternative to the Socratic-Hegelian point of view is essentially what Kierkegaard himself affirms. In these texts Kierkegaard "argues for" his understanding of the Christian faith by having Johannes, as a neutral observer, spell out its difference from views sometimes claiming identity with it. When I speak of Johannes's critique as Kierkegaard's view, I am assuming this relation between the two.

[4]*PF*, 53-54 and *CUP*, 327-28.

[5]*PF*, 225-26 in the older edition cited in n. 2 above, and *Luther's Works*, 26:230. Cf. 12:346 on "the battle that human reason wages against the sentences of God." For Luther's view of reason I draw only on his 1535 *Lectures on Galatians* and his 1538 *Commentary on Psalm 51*, delivered as lectures, respectively, in 1531 and 1532. The former is found in *Luther's Works*, vol. 26-27, Jaroslav Pelikan and Walter A. Hansen, eds. (St. Louis: Concordia, 1963-1964), while the latter is found in vol. 12, Jaroslav Pelikan, ed., 1955.

[6]*Luther's Works*, 26:64 and 12:303.

[7]Ibid., 26:113, 120, 156-57, 307, 368; 27:6-7, 56; 26:64, 215-16, 233, 268; 27:54.

[8]See especially the summary of the Pauline view in *Theological Dictionary of the New Testament*, Gerhard Friedrich, ed., and Geoffrey W. Bromiley, trans. (Grand Rapids: Eerdmans, 1971) 7:135; and Rudolph Bultmann, *Theology of the New Testament*, Kendrick Grobel, trans. (New York: Scribner's, 1951) 1:232-46.

informed by, and independent of, the Word and Spirit of God. It is by no means unreligious, but its religion is based on the presumption of self-chosen forms of worship, and these deserve to be called superstition.[9]

That reason can be an expression of the flesh is the simple corollary of Luther's doctrine of total depravity. This doctrine is concerned with the extent of sin, not its intensity. Luther does not assert that we are as evil as we can be, but rather that no part of us has escaped the corrupting and distorting impact of the Fall. More specifically, he means that our intellect is sinfully estranged from the truth of God just as our will is sinfully estranged from God's goodness. Blinded by sin, reason is blind to sin. Reason does not recognize its seriousness nor its power in human life. Furthermore, its vision of sin is selective. It knows that murder, theft, and adultery are sin, but does not clearly perceive the sins of decent, good, and even saintly folk.[10]

This explains why reason is an ally of the flesh and the law but an enemy of the spirit and the gospel. The message of sin and grace that Luther finds to be the heart of the Christian evangel stands in the logical relation of contrary or contradictory to reason. Reason finds the gospel to be "absurd" and a "paradox." But these merely logical categories are inadequate to the full humanness of reason. In the presence of absurdity and paradox, reason is "offended." It sounds as if Luther has been reading Johannes Climacus.[11]

It must not be overlooked that Luther is not speaking of reason *simpliciter*. In the same texts that contain his sustained polemic against reason, Luther is able to complain that those who are under "the bewitchment of the devil" and do not accept the gospel "do not listen to reason; they do not admit Scripture." Thus Luther distinguishes "right reason," the "reason of faith," informed by the word of the gospel from the reason that is offended at the gospel and flees from God through sin.[12] This is why he so frequently adds a verbal qualifier and speaks of "natural reason" or, more frequently, of "human reason" when describing the intellect as an expression of the flesh and a passionate (offended) enemy of the gospel.

Sin as an Epistemological Category in Johannes's Thought Experiment

The Lutheran idea of Reason being offended at the Christian gospel on the grounds of its absurd and paradoxical appearance lies at the very heart of the thought experiment in *Philosophical Fragments*. However, before studying this experiment it will be useful to place the *Philosophical Fragments* in the context of the

---

[9]*Luther's Works*, 26:235, 375; 27:54; 12:304, 314, 321; 26:173, 229, 309, 396-97; 27:54-57.

[10]Ibid., 26:174-75; 27:53; 12:323, 341-42; 26:33-34, 340-41.

[11]Ibid., 26:159, 290, 161, 227, 231, 214, 305, 419, 421; 27:56.

[12]Ibid., 26:194, 323, 262.

pseudonymous authorship. It would be entirely correct to say that *Fear and Trembling* addresses the ethical or practical meaning of faith. Through reflections on the Abraham story, Kierkegaard launches a critique of the demonic tendency of human society to absolutize itself by making itself the ultimate frame of reference for human life. The satire on the idea of going "beyond faith" that forms the frame for reflections on Abraham raises epistemological questions about the nature of faith in the context of the Hegelian movement from *Vorstellung* to *Begriff*.[13] What remains to be done is to give a more general account of the epistemological issues and to link them to ethicopolitical issues overtly through the concept of legitimation. These tasks are begun in the *Fragments* and carried further in the *Postscript*.

The immediate purpose of this experiment is to discover whether there is a cogent alternative to the Socratic theory of knowledge as recollection. In keeping with the fundamental intentions of Socrates, Kierkegaard takes the issue not to be the truth of everyday facts such as the time of day or of sophisticated scientific theories such as quantum mechanics, but the ethicoreligious Truth—a Janus-faced truth that looks both toward the nature of ultimate reality, the Eternal, and toward the personal question of how I should live my life.[14] The Socratic theory is that this Truth is already within us. This would not mean (with the slave boy from the *Meno* in the background) that we have consciously formulated the Truth for ourselves already or that we can produce the Truth upon demand; in either case the metaphor of forgetting and remembering would lose its force. Instead it means that we are able to recognize the Truth as the Truth when presented with it, an ability Johannes calls "the condition." I may not be able to remember the name of that redheaded kid with the beautiful smile from my fourth-grade class, but if you give me a list of the names of students in the class, I'll pick it out right away.

The thought experiment that searches for an alternative to this perspective is no idle game. It has a target, and that target, of course, is not Socrates but Hegel, Hegelian intellectuals, and a Christendom of which they are the all-too-adequate expression. It is important to notice that these are the same target that Kierkegaard aimed at in *Fear and Trembling*. The thought experiment will be damaging to them if there is a cogent alternative to Socrates and if this includes an unmistakably Christian cluster of concepts. From the point of view of Kierkegaard's target, Christianity and the Socratic theory are identical rather than alternatives expressing a stark either/or.

Hegel himself expressed the Socratic idea in a fragmentary essay from his seminary days in Tübingen. "Even if their authority rests on a divine revelation the doctrines must necessarily be so constituted that they are authorized really by the universal Reason of mankind, so that every man sees and feels

---

[13]Regarding these points, see "Abraham and Hegel," ch. 5, especially the last half.

[14]For explicit statements of what is contextually clear in the *Fragments,* see not only the *Postscript* but also *PV,* 110 and 115.

their obligatory force when it is drawn to his attention."[15] Kierkegaard could not have known this text, but he was perceptive enough to see that its thought was fundamental to the entire Hegelian project, in particular to the claim that his philosophy had the same content as the Christian religion, differing only in form. For the central meaning of the transition from *Vorstellung* to *Begriff* is not the elimination of images from thought but the elimination of the external relation presupposed between the human self and the Divine should the Truth not be within us. Johannes puts it this way: "In the Socratic view each individual is his own center, and the entire world centers in him, because his self-knowledge is a knowledge of God." Because he understood this, Socrates "had the courage and the self-possession to be sufficient unto himself, but also in his relations to his fellowmen to be merely an occasion."[16] This is the meaning of the Greek idea that the soul is divine.

But sin and a divine human soul do not go together conceptually. Sin is the notion that evil does not come from the body or somewhere outside one's real self but rather from the very core of one's centered being, which thereby shows itself to be anything but divine.[17] It is not surprising that sin turns up almost immediately in the search for an alternative to the Socratic assumption that the Truth is within us. If we are devoid of the Truth in the requisite, strong sense of lacking even the condition of recognizing it, then we must be "beyond the pale of the Truth" and "in a state of Error."[18]

By itself this condition exhibits our lack of divinity, but in the context of the biblical faith that Kierkegaard seeks to evoke here, we are doubly different from divinity by virtue of the creation and of the Fall. Johannes proceeds immediately to indicate that it is the latter that accounts for our being in Error. "In so far as [we exist as learners we are] already created, and hence God must have endowed [us] with the condition for understanding the Truth." If we are now lacking this condition we must have lost it subsequent to our creation. But "this deprivation cannot have been due to an act of the God (which would have been a contradiction), nor to an accident (for it would be a contradiction to assume that the lower could overcome the higher); it must therefore be due to [ourselves]. . . . But this state of being in Error by reason of [our] own guilt, what shall we call it? Let us call it *Sin*."[19] Admittedly this is

---

[15]From a fragmentary essay of 1793, translated in the appendix to H.S. Harris, *Hegel's Development: Toward the Sunlight, 1770-1801* (Oxford: Clarendon Press, 1972) 499.

[16]*PF*, 11.

[17]In his *Confessions* Augustine makes the absence of this concept of sin the crucial flaw of the Manichee faith from a Christian point of view. Of course, at one time it was just this feature that made that faith so useful to him in justifying a life that he knew violated his own ethical ideals. See 4:15; 5:10; 7:3; 8:10; and 9:4.

[18]*PF*, 13-14.

[19]Ibid., 15. His italics.

the sketchiest of arguments, but there is no ambiguity about its point, on which the remainder of the discussion depends.

We will not rightly interpret Johannes's account of Reason and the Paradox in the *Fragments* if we overlook that sin, and not finitude, lies at the crux of the issue. Unfortunately, the text itself often seems to be an invitation to just that forgetting. In order to keep the structure of the argument clearly before us, we might well borrow a schema from the *Postscript*, which reminds us that "sin is the decisive expression for the religious mode of existence," taking us beyond what can only be described as "merely the discrepancy of the finite and the infinite."[20] Just as there are three expressions of existential pathos in the *Postscript*, so there are three expressions of the Paradox in the writings of Johannes. The *initial expression* of the Paradox remains within the *metaphysical* domain. It is God simply as God who is paradoxical to (finite) human understanding. In its *essential expression* the Paradox becomes a *metaphysically confessional* issue. It is God incarnate, not simply the Eternal, but the Eternal in time that is paradoxical to (finite) human understanding. In its *decisive expression* the Paradox becomes a *personally confessional* issue. It is God on the cross who is offensive to (sinful) human understanding. God incarnate is by virtue of true incarnation exposed to suffering and death. Incarnation is not epiphany. But that this suffering and death should be on account of our sins is a wholly different matter.

As we proceed toward the decisive expression of the Paradox we pass from the finitude of a human understanding that has conceptual problems with God as the Eternal, and with God as the Eternal in time, to the sinfulness of a human understanding that has existential problems with the notion that Christ died for our sins. This is the point at which the Paradox moves from absurdity to offense, at which it becomes possible to understand how Luther could see human reason as an expression of the flesh. For this is the point at which repentance is an indispensable condition for hearing the Christian story of God's love as good news. Needless to say, it is this sort of juncture between intellect and interest, concept and desire, toward which the hermeneutics of suspicion is directed.[21]

---

[20]*CUP*, 239.

[21]Thus Paul Ricoeur says that "representation obeys not only a law of intentionality which makes it the expression of some object, but also another law, which makes it the manifestation of life, of an effort or desire. It is because of the interference of the latter expressive function that representation can be distorted. Thus representation may be investigated in two ways: on the one hand, by a gnoseology (or criteriology) according to which representation is viewed as an intentional relation ruled by objects that manifest themselves in that intentionality, and on the other hand by an exegesis of the desires that lie hidden in that intentionality." Through the suspicion that reminds us of this "nonautonomy of knowledge" we discover "not only the unsurpassable nature of life, but the interference of desire with intentionality, upon which desire inflicts an invincible obscurity, an ineluctable partiality." *Freud and Philosophy*, 457-58.

After introducing sin as an epistemological category in chapter 1 of the *Fragments*, Johannes explores the paradoxical nature of faith in the remaining chapters. Since this involves all three dimensions of the Paradox, there are times when attention to either its initial expression or its essential expression makes it easy for us to forget the decisiveness of the decisive expression. Johannes regularly reminds us not to lose sight of the whole while exploring the parts.

Much of chapter 2 revolves around a beautiful parable that Johannes introduces with these words, "Suppose there was a king who loved a humble maiden."[22] The problem of the lovers is how to overcome the difference between them so that true intimacy will be possible. At first glance this difference is one of rank. The varying social strata in the parable represent the metaphysical difference between Creator and creature in real life. We are dealing with the initial dimension of the Paradox, the utter difference between God and even the highest of His created beings. Casting his parable aside, Johannes proceeds to the essential expression of the Paradox. God's strategy will be to become human, to bridge the gap by taking the form of a servant. This servant form will have to be "no mere outer garment," which means that God will become capable of suffering and even of death.[23] To repeat, we are led to the concept of incarnation, not epiphany. That a god should appear in human form is a wonder indeed, but that a god should actually become a human being so as to win our love without deceiving or destroying us, that is quite paradoxical.

In the meantime, what has happened to sin? A careless reading would suggest that for Johannes the Paradox is primarily speculative and conceptual, located in the metaphysical and metaphysically confessional ideas of God the creator and God incarnate respectively. A careful reading will show that these themes do not stand alone, but are part of a context that gives them their fully existential meaning. Such a context, of course, is that of human sin, the reminder that God's being is paradoxical to me because I would like to be the ultimate power and authority that the Creator rightfully is. Moreover, the Incarnation is paradoxical to me because I can only rejoice in it through repentance.

Three times in chapter 2 Johannes reminds the reader of this context. The first two times we are reminded that as learners we are in Error through our own guilt and thus the dissimilitude between ourselves and God that makes it so difficult for us to understand him is not just the metaphysical difference of inferiority but more basically the moral difference of insubordination. This explains why Johannes so strongly stresses the inadequacy of the parable to its subject matter.[24] For in the story of the king and the humble maiden, there

---

[22]*PF*, 26.

[23]Ibid., 31-34.

[24]Ibid., 28, 31, 25-26.

is no suggestion that the maiden's loyalty is with the guerillas seeking his overthrow.

The third reminder occurs in a discussion of the Incarnation. Because the servant form is no mere outer garment, the God in time is vulnerable to a life of suffering and eventually to death. How paradoxical. If death is more bitter than wormwood for mortals, how much more bitter for an *immortal*. But this is death on a cross, and the paradox is that he who dies as one who is guilty is in fact the only one who is *innocent*. That the immortal should die is puzzling enough, but that the innocent should die for the guilty, the just for the unjust, that is more than puzzling. The difference between mortal and immortal is immediately *aufgehoben* in the difference between the guilty and the innocent.[25] The metaphysical difference between ourselves and the Teacher is mentioned only to be taken up immediately into the ontological difference. From the view Johannes is exploring we get to the very being of the learner only with the category of sin.

Chapter 3 of the *Fragments* evokes the initial expression of the Paradox in discussing the project of proving the existence of God. The atmosphere is distinctly Kantian, with the finitude of human reason in the foreground. Like a moth ineluctably drawn toward the flames that will destroy it, Reason is portrayed as a passion seeking to collide with its limit by discovering "something that thought cannot think." In an evidently deliberate evocation of the opening lines of the *Critique of Pure Reason,* Johannes tells us that in relation to this limit, the Unknown, "Reason cannot advance beyond this point, and yet it cannot refrain in its paradoxicalness from arriving at this limit and occupying itself therewith."[26] Like Kant, Johannes indicates that we are dealing with the question of God, but unlike Kant his generic account of the abyss in which Reason founders is not "the unconditioned" but rather "the absolutely different . . . an absolute unlikeness."[27] Reason cannot think what is wholly other than itself, just as the humble maiden could not understand the king due to his different station.

By virtue of this absolute difference, Paradox becomes the Absolute Paradox in chapter 3; but wherein does this absolute unlikeness consist? Once again Johannes is utterly unambiguous. It consists not in our created fini-

---

[25]Ibid., 34. Johannes is tracing the argument of Paul in Romans 5:6-10. To get the full force of the idea that "Christ died for the ungodly," Paul notes that this death occurred "while we were yet helpless," then "while we were yet sinners," and finally "while we were [God's] enemies" (RSV).

[26]*PF,* 37, 44. The opening sentence of the preface to the first edition of the *Critique of Pure Reason* reads as follows: "Human reason has this peculiar fate that in one species of its knowledge it is burdened by questions which, as prescribed by the very nature of reason itself, it is not able to ignore, but which, as transcending all its powers, it is also not able to answer" (Norman Kemp Smith translation).

[27]*PF,* 39-40, 45.

Merold Westphal

tude, but in our fallen sinfulness. The Paradox becomes absolute by virtue of its decisive expression. "But if the God and man are absolutely different, this cannot be accounted for on the basis of what man derives from the God, for in so far they are akin. Their unlikeness must therefore be explained by what man derives from himself, or by what he has brought upon his own head. But what can this unlikeness be? Aye, what can it be but sin; since the unlikeness, the absolute unlikeness, is something that man has brought upon himself. We have expressed this in the preceding by saying that man was in Error, and had brought this upon his head by his own guilt." From this perspective Ricoeur's rhetorical question is all but unavoidable: "Does not sin make God the Wholly Other?"[28] Johannes's account of natural theology is eventually less Kantian than Pauline. He portrays Reason not as the weakness of finite humanity but as the wrongness of fallen humanity, "who by their wickedness suppress the truth" and thereby become "futile in their thinking."[29]

At this point Johannes suggests that faith be seen not as an alternative to knowledge but as the alternative to offense.[30] In relation to the Absolute Paradox, Reason shows itself to be Offended Consciousness. It shouts loudly about its incompatibility with the Paradox, but manages only to produce an acoustic illusion, presenting as its own discovery a mere echo of what the Paradox has already said about its relation to Reason (fallen, human reason).[31]

Chapters 4 and 5 contain a long discussion of the God in time, returning to the essential expression of the Paradox. One passage seems to restrict the issue to this level. "If the contemporary generation had left nothing behind them but these words: 'We have believed that in such and such a year that God appeared among us in the humble figure of a servant, that he lived and taught in our community, and finally died,' it would be more than enough." Nevertheless, by now we are confident that Johannes will not let us drop the decisive expression from view, and he does not disappoint us. He reminds us that the idea of the Incarnation is not only a *"folly to the understanding"*

---

[28]Ibid., 46-47 and Paul Ricoeur, *The Symbolism of Evil,* Emerson Buchanan, trans. (New York: Harper, 1967) 58. Rudolf Otto moves in the same direction in "The Holy as a Category of Value," in *The Idea of the Holy,* John W. Harvey, trans. (New York: Oxford University Press, 1958). He insists that "the meaning of 'sin' is not understood by the 'natural,' or even by the merely moral, man," and adds that "rationalism lacked understanding of what 'sin' is" (52-53). Similarly Johannes notes that what Socrates lacks is precisely "the consciousness of sin" (*PF,* 47).

[29]Romans 1:18-23 (RSV).

[30]*PF,* 49-59.

[31]In this connection it is useful to read the sermon on 1 Corinthians 2:6-9, which Kierkegaard preached at Trinity Church, Copenhagen, in February 1844 while he was working on the *Fragments.* See *Johannes Climacus or, De Omnibus Dubitandum Est and A Sermon,* T. H. Croxall, trans. (Stanford: Stanford University Press, 1958) 159-73.

but also *"an offense to the human heart."* If we remember what is involved in his understanding of offense, we will not be surprised to find him also reminding us that both the contemporary disciple and the disciple at second hand are subject to the same epistemological predicament, sin; and the same epistemological salvation, the grace of God that grants the condition is available to both of them. Thus faith is "equally difficult" and "equally easy" for them.[32] Differences of intellect and historical location are essentially irrelevant. Sin is the great equalizer.

How the Thought Experiment of the *Fragments* Becomes Ideology Critique in the *Postscript*

It is clear that by making sin the decisive factor in the Paradox Johannes has introduced sin as an epistemological category.[33] This is, in turn, an invitation to the hermeneutics of suspicion, for if Reason is an expression of the flesh, one's belief dispositions will be anything but innocent.[34] Instead, the foundations of one's intellect will include motivations that cannot be acknowledged. Self-examination in the spirit of Thomas à Kempis becomes a noetic imperative.

But where is the spirit of Karl Marx in all this, previously alleged to be wed by Johannes to the spirit of Thomas à Kempis? The notion of ideology critique means more than suspicion about the motivations that keep Reason from being pure. It involves the notion that the rationality in question is both historically specific and socially functional. In other words, rationality secretly serves special interests by providing legitimation for the particular society whose acceptance of it enables it to wear the honorific title, Reason. But this title is more than honorific. By its overtones of universal and timeless necessity, it masks the particular and contingent interests that govern the thinking of those who use reason. In religious societies the ideas that legitimize will be called Revelation, whether this refers to mythological or historical narratives. In secular societies the ideas that legitimize will be called Reason. In the *Fragments* we have seen Johannes unwilling to be intimidated by certain ideas that are called Reason. But, to repeat the question, where are the elements that would make that unwillingness into ideology critique?

---

[32]*PF*, 103, 102, 106-107.

[33]Note the reprise at *CUP*, 184-91.

[34]This locution is used by Nick Wolterstorff in the development of what has come to be called "Reformed" or "Calvinian" epistemology. With reference to both Marx and Freud, he speaks of "ignoble" and "noninnocent" belief dispositions, and affirms that these "dispositions are signs of our fallenness, not part of our pristine nature." See "Can Belief in God Be Rational If It Has No Foundations?" in *Faith and Rationality: Reason and Belief in God,* Alvin Plantinga and Nicholas Wolterstorff, eds. (Notre Dame: University of Notre Dame Press, 1983) 149, 163, and 174.

The most direct answer is that they are in the *Postscript*. There Johannes addresses such questions as, "How has sin shaped the thinking of the modern age?" and "How has contemporary society managed to deceive itself about this so as to be at peace with its conscience?"

But already in the preface to the *Fragments* we are, in effect, promised such a sequel and challenged to read it between the lines of the *Fragments*. The preface announces that the work to follow is an untimely meditation, without "the slightest pretention to share in the philosophical movement of the day." Johannes assimilates his "failure to serve the system" with the kind of "offense against the State" exhibited by Sallust and Socrates, whose virtues estranged them from the socially prevailing theory and practice of the good life. He then evokes Archimedes and Diogenes, who even in a moment of military crisis ironically found that what the age demands is not necessarily ultimate. The nonmilitary project Johannes begs to be excused from is designated on the one hand by the slogans, "a new era," "a new epoch," and "the system," and on the other hand by "ease and security in life, such as is implied in having a wife and children," and that allows entry into "the domestic happiness, the civic respectability, the glad fellowship, the *communio bonorum*" that entitles one to have opinions that are taken seriously.[35] Kierkegaard's target is plainly a particular set of ideas and the society that has adopted these ideas as its own. It is Hegel and the "almost Hegelian public" whose thinking he will challenge.[36]

The *Postscript* also begins with a preface that emphasizes its incongruity with "the seething ferment of the times" because Johannes has "no overhasty concern for what the times demand." He is not indebted, and therefore not enslaved, to those who speak so decisively for the age that their approval would make his book important. So it should come as no surprise when he finally says that he is attacking "the specific immorality of the age."[37] For Paul and Luther sin may be a generic, permanent feature of fallen humanity in all historical settings, with the result that their theological critique of human reason never gains the historical specificity of ideology critique. This is not the case for Johannes.[38] His target is not sinful, human rationality *überhaupt*, but the

---

[35]*PF*, 5-7.

[36]*CUP*, 34.

[37]Ibid., 3-6, 317.

[38]For the difference between Luther's view of the social order as essentially expressive of the divine order of creation and Kierkegaard's lack of any such confidence in the status quo, see Johannes Sløk, "Kierkegaard and Luther," in *A Kierkegaard Critique*, Howard A. Johnson and Niels Thulstrup, eds. (Chicago: Henry Regnery, 1962) 92-93 and 97-100. In Luther's view the content of right behavior is present in my station and its duties, the only question being whether, in terms of inwardness, I do the right thing in the obedience of faith. For Kierkegaard, by contrast, since his account of inwardness has a social critique built right into it, the question cannot be simply whether I do the duties of my station for the right motives, for my station has been defined in terms of a Reason essentially contaminated by sin.

dominant ideas of his own age: mid-nineteenth-century liberal, national, industrial Christendom.[39]

It may be difficult to read the *Postscript* as ideology critique and thus to feel the spirit of Marx in it because it is so manifestly not a critique of political economy.[40] But why should it be? Johannes does not think capitalism is "the specific immorality of the age." In his view the "characteristic depravity" of his own society is

> a dissolute pantheistic contempt for the individual. . . . In the midst of all our exultation over the achievements of the age and the nineteenth century, there sounds a note of poorly conceived contempt for the individual . . . in the midst of the self-importance of the contemporary generation there is revealed a sense of despair over being human. . . . No one wants to be an individual human being. . . . Just as desert travellers combine into great caravans from fear of robbers and wild beasts, so the individuals of the contemporary generation are fearful of existence, because it is God-forsaken; only in great masses do they dare to live, and they cluster together *en masse* in order to feel that they amount to something.

The cause and effect of this is that human life is lived outside the ethical and religious spheres.[41]

Modern, mass society has its own individualism. As an age that is "liberal, broad-minded, and philosophical," it supports "the sacred claims of personal liberty." But the individualism of the *Postscript* is directed against this individualism and the collectivism that is the other side of the same modern coin.[42] It is important to note that whatever the individualism of the *Postscript* may mean, it is so far from expressing an apolitical or asocial attitude on Kierkegaard's part that it lies at the very heart of his critique of modern society.

There is a second crucial point to be noted about the "contempt for the individual" that Johannes finds to be the "characteristic depravity" of modernity. We could say that from his perspective the "specific immorality" of the age is its amorality. The deepest meaning of modernity in the *Postscript* is its

---

[39]For a very helpful account of Kierkegaard's social and cultural setting, see John W. Elrod, *Kierkegaard and Christendom* (Princeton: Princeton University Press, 1981) esp. chs. 1 and 2.

[40]It is important to notice that ideology critique is an indirect form of social criticism. By comparison with Engels' *The Condition of the Working Class in England,* the critique of political economy that Marx worked on from the 1844 manuscripts through *Capital* was an indirect attack upon capitalist society by means of a critique of the theory that legitimized it. The *Postscript* is ideology critique by virtue of its criticism of the theory of the modern age.

[41]*CUP,* 317-18. Cf. my discussion of these passages in "Kierkegaard's Politics," ch. 3.

[42]Ibid., 4. For a comparison of Kierkegaard's dialectical individualism with the compositional individualism of modern liberal thought, see "Kierkegaard's Politics," ch. 3.

objectivity, its exclusion of the subjectivity and inwardness that are definitive of the ethical and religious spheres of existence. Kierkegaard's theory of the stages or spheres of existence is a form of transcendental philosophy. It seeks to articulate the categorical systems that are conditions for the possibility of various modes of human experience. To say that the modern age has contempt for the individual who is defined by the subjectivity and inwardness of the ethical and religious spheres is to say that the transcendental subjectivity of modernity, its categorical framework, its theory of all theories, is not merely secular but beyond good and evil. Because the basic categories of the ethical are not part of its repertoire, Johannes must find the specific immorality of the age to be its amorality.

As preparation for looking at how this develops into ideology critique in the *Postscript* it may be useful to consider briefly the link between a preethical, transcendental subjectivity and the legitimation of modernity in the thought of Jürgen Habermas. By his analysis the classical doctrine of politics was a branch of ethics, concerning itself with the right and the just, with virtue and freedom. It was a *phronesis* intended to guide *praxis*. But modern political science is a *techne* intended to guide *poiesis*. In both cases political knowledge is meant to be the theory of the good life, a guide to happiness, but in the process the meanings of these key terms, good life and happiness, have changed radically. In classical thought they were essentially linked to the concept of virtue, while in modern thought they relate to the satisfaction of pre-ethical desire.[43]

This also involves a change in the concept of reason. Instead of being a participatory insight into the point at which being and value are inseparable, it becomes the calculation of effective and efficient means of achieving given ends. This instrumental reason can provide technical rules or recommendations for control of the natural and human environment (rules of skill and counsels of prudence in Kantian language), but it cannot provide valid norms for action (categorical imperatives).[44] Although it can tell us how to be effective (how to achieve our ends) and how to be efficient (how to achieve them at the least cost to ourselves), it has nothing at all to say about what ends we

---

[43]See "The Classical Doctrine of Politics in Relation to Social Philosophy," in *Theory and Practice,* John Viertel, trans. (Boston: Beacon Press, 1973). Henceforth *TP*. The same point that Habermas develops here in Aristotelian categories he develops in Hegelian categories in "Labor and Interaction: Remarks on Hegel's Jena *Philosophy of Mind* "(also in *TP*).

[44]*Toward a Rational Society: Student Protest, Science, and Politics,* Jeremy J. Shapiro, trans. (Boston: Beacon Press, 1970) 55-56, and *Legitimation Crisis,* Thomas McCarthy, trans. (Boston: Beacon Press, 1975) 10. Henceforth *TRS* and *LC,* respectively. This is not to say that instrumental reason is without any norms at all. It is rather to speak of "the problematic origin of the norms of natural reason in the mechanics of natural desires" (*TP*, 62). What is problematic about this origin, of course, is the absence of any moral constraints upon human desire or the means of satisfying it.

should pursue or what means we may *not* employ in their pursuit. Since the answers to these questions will inevitably be arbitrary, instrumental reason is linked to what Habermas calls "decisionism."[45] "Rationality in the choice of means accompanies avowed irrationality in orientation to values, goals, and needs."[46] The worst thing reason could say about society is that it is "poorly programmed."[47]

Within the framework of instrumental reason *"practical substance is eliminated. . . .* It eliminates practical questions and therewith precludes discussion about the adoption of standards."[48] Since these standards are the basis for ethical questions about what ends we ought to pursue and what means we may not employ in the pursuit of legitimate ends, the technocratic consciousness of instrumental reason "reflects not the sundering of an ethical situation but the *repression of 'ethics' as such as a category of life.*"[49]

For Habermas as for Kierkegaard modernity's Reason has become amoral. Moreover, this is directly linked to the process of legitimation in Habermas's view. He distinguishes legitimation from above and below, invoking the Marxian spatial metaphor of the economic system as the foundation, the political system as the first floor of the superstructure, and the cultural system as the second floor. Traditional societies are legitimized from above. This is to say that the economic and political systems are authorized from the cultural realm in terms of an understanding of the cosmos as a whole. This understanding can be religious, expressed in mythological and/or historical narratives, or philosophical, expressed in arguments. But the transition from traditional to modern society changes legitimation. The religious and philosophical traditions lose their power as the rise of historical consciousness enables them to be seen *as* traditions. More importantly, capitalism creates a situation in which it becomes possible for society to be legitimized from below, for the rationality of the economic system to justify the political and cultural system it supports and is supported by.[50]

---

[45]*TRS,* 80; *TP,* 46.

[46]*TRS,* 63. Cf. 82. Habermas quotes Lübbe's account of the decisionist context in which "the politician takes positions in conflict situations for which there is no court of earthly reason" (*TRS,* 65). If the arbitrariness this involves were fully avowed, as suggested in the passage on 63, there would be no need for a hermeneutics of suspicion to uncover it, a hermeneutics modeled since *Knowledge and Human Interests* on Freudian psychoanalysis. In practice, I believe, Habermas keeps to this model and, like MacIntyre in *After Virtue,* treats modernity as being committed to an arbitrariness (decisionism, emotivism) that it is only rarely and incompletely able to avow.

[47]*TRS,* 84.

[48]Ibid., 103. His italics.

[49]Ibid., 112. My italics.

[50]Ibid., 53-54, 81-83, 95-100. See also *Communication and the Evolution of Society,*

At first this new legitimation retains a moral dimension, since the market, in terms of which everything else is justified, is itself justified in terms of justice, the exchange of equivalents.[51] Whether or not this view of things was ever deservedly convincing, it does not survive the transition from liberal to advanced capitalism. With or without help from Marx, the emergence of social legislation and the rise of the welfare state gives testimony to the injustice of the market exchange between labor and capital. Moreover, the growth of state involvement in the economy through planning, welfare expenditures, military expenditures, and so forth, makes it increasingly unrealistic to talk about the market as if it were free. The result is that legitimation from below loses its moral character entirely. Society still justifies itself as a whole in terms of its system of production; and yet the moral features of that system are no longer relevant. It is not the justice of capitalist production, but its productivity that matters. It produces security and prosperity, in short, happiness as the uncritical satisfaction of preethical desires. This is what makes it worthwhile.[52]

Max Weber's concept of rationalization is an attempt to understand modernity in terms of its new rationality. He spells this out in terms of value-free, instrumental thought and its power to guide purpose-rational action. Perhaps the reason he is so uncritical of this process is that while he was aware of the secularization it involved, the "disenchantment" of the world, he did not fully realize the import of reason's being freed from the spell of morality at the same time and given over to the arbitrary power of whatever sophistry or soldiery might impose. It is precisely this amorality of modernity's Reason that Habermas sees as the legitimation crisis of our times.[53]

That is Kierkegaard's view as well, though he comes to it via Hegel rather than Weber. In the *Postscript* he analyzes the amoral rationality in terms of which the modern age sanctifies itself. This analysis is ideology critique because it seeks to expose the self-deception in modernity's social self-justification, to reveal the contradiction between modernity's amoral operative rationality and its by no means amoral self-image as cultured and Christian.

Johannes calls modernity's Reason objectivity. Schleiermacher reassures the cultured despisers of religion that there is nothing offensive about true religion and Hegel nearly agrees, promising that any offensive elements will

---

Thomas McCarthy, trans. (Boston: Beacon Press, 1979) 183-85. Habermas's own attempt to reinstate the ethical dimension into social legitimation through formalist or procedural means links his thought to that of John Rawls in a way that deserves attention. We could learn a lot about Kierkegaard's thought by staging a three-way conversation between Kierkegaard, Habermas, and Rawls.

[51] *TRS,* 97; *LC,* 26.

[52] *TRS,* 82-83; *LC,* 73-75, 93, 123, Cf. Hannah Arendt's interpretation (in *On Revolution*) of modernity as the triumph of happiness over freedom, where 'happiness' has taken on its distinctively amoral sense as prosperity, security, etc.

[53] *TRS,* 81.

be eliminated as intellectuals translate Christianity from its popular form (*Vorstellung*) to its cultured form (*Begriff*). But Johannes sees the objectivity that is the pride of the cultured as "the sin of intellect," which, by exempting them from the "labor of inwardness," constantly causes "resistance against becoming a Christian." He tells us that the sequel to the *Fragments* "was to be devoted to the task of investing the problem in historical costume."[54] The "historical costume" for the problem of the noetic effects of sin is the analysis of objectivity in the *Postscript*. According to this analysis objectivity has several generic characteristics and two specific modes of expression in Kierkegaard's world, orthodoxy and speculative philosophy.

The entry into objectivity is through *disinterestedness*. The goal is *certainty*. The reward is *security*.[55] These generic features of objectivity represent not so much the primacy of theory over practice (in Johannes's view objectivity is a theoretical posture in the service of a practice freed from "the labor of inwardness") as the primacy of a particular theory of theory and thus the practice of a particular cognitive attitude, scientific detachment. What gets left behind as we enter the sphere of objectivity is action grounded in the inwardness that characterizes the ethical and religious spheres. For such action occurs in the realm where knowledge is essentially related to the knower. Thus, instead of being disinterested, it grows out of an "infinite personal passionate interest." This passion is incompatible with utter certainty. It follows, of course, that the realm of subjectivity cannot be a realm of security. Faith is unavoidably a risk, a venture. Objectivity is the amorality of modern Reason.[56]

Speculative philosophy (in the Hegelian tradition) and theological orthodoxy (in the Lutheran tradition) are the two specific embodiments of objectivity that Kierkegaard sees as dominant in his society. They unite to reassure a society whose operative rationality places it outside the realms of ethics and religion altogether that it is nevertheless still Christian. Through this self-deception, self-respect (even to the point of self-righteousness) is maintained.

The fundamental contradiction of speculative philosophy (meaning, of course, the Hegelian tradition and not, for example, the traditions of Socrates and Lessing) is that philosophy is objectivity while Christianity is subjectivity. Yet it claims to be not merely Christian, but the ultimately improved edition of Christianity. With special reference to its orientation to world history, Johannes refutes these claims by noting that the system has no ethics. It is not even playing in the ballpark where Christianity might be encountered.[57]

The system has no ethics by virtue of its basic categories, its point of view, and its point of reference. Just as the aesthete stands outside the realm of eth-

---

[54]*CUP*, 536, 14.

[55]Ibid., 23-24, 282-84, 30, 70-71, 379, 406.

[56]Ibid., 269-72, 177, 53, 30, 407, 182, 188, 384.

[57]Ibid., 117, 192-201, 108-10.

icoreligious subjectivity by virtue of the priority of categories of "the boring"
and "the interesting" in the aesthetic view of life, so the speculative philosopher neutralizes "the absolute ethical distinction between good and evil" by
giving primacy to the categories of "the great" and "the significant." What
makes a person historically important is quite "accidental" from the ethical
point of view. The categories of "fortune" and "misfortune" also come to the
fore, likewise shifting attention from inwardness to outwardness. Everything
depends on the consequences of our action, and the importance of intention,
purpose, and motive fades from view. In this way the concept of sin is effectively eliminated, and the human failure becomes, not depravity and corruption, but weakness and imperfection. We are reminded of Richard Nixon, who
admits that Watergate represented a foolish mistake on his part, but who to
this day refuses to apply ethical categories to his behavior. In response to the
suggestion that room remains in the kingdom of consequences for an ethic
of prudence, Johannes replies that "the ethical never raises questions of prudence," that we would be unwise to trust those for whom honesty is the best
policy.[58]

The system's point of view is also beyond good and evil, and in two ways.
Its world-historical concern for the past and its sense of affinity with the eternal through recollection free it from subjectivity's orientation toward the future. It adopts the perspective of spectator rather than responsible agent. Life
ceases to be seen as an ethicoreligious task. The real subject is the knowing
subject. It's as if the system were saying, "Before me thinkers only tried to
change the world; the task, however, is to understand it differently."[59]

The second way in which the system's point of view is beyond good and
evil is that it poses not as any spectator of human history but as the divine
spectator.[60] Whether it is the individual or the age that practices this "ungodly
and pantheistic self-deification," the result is the same—the elimination of
the ethical frame of reference. For the condition of the possibility of ethicoreligious subjectivity and inwardness is the position of the human subject, individual or corporate, before God in a relation of nonidentity. In fact,
inwardness is defined in just these terms: "Inwardness is the relationship of
the individual to himself before God."[61] From the divine perspective not only
does the Paradox disappear from view but also the category of sin that be-

[58]Ibid., 120, 139, 388, 391, 430, 480, 121, 139, 144, 240, 125.

[59]Ibid., 44, 131, 272-73, 146-47, 281.

[60]Ibid., 44, 107-108, 126, 141, 354.

[61]Ibid., 122, 139-41, 391. This is why Anti-Climacus, Johannes's successor, will write
that "every individual ought to live in fear and trembling, and so too there is no established order which can do without fear and trembling," since "fear and trembling signifies that a God exists—a fact which no man and no established order dare for an
instant forget" (TC, 89).

longs essentially to it. God is not sinfully paradoxical to himself, either as maker of heaven and earth or as suffering servant.[62]

Finally, the system has no ethics by virtue of its point of reference. It confuses itself not only with God but with humanity at large. In doing so it elevates the race over the individual and adopts as its ultimate criterion "what the age demands."[63] When a society or an era makes itself its ultimate point of reference, this can only be an expression of self-deification. But there is an ironical dialectic to this process, which Johannes expresses by saying that the "great secret of the System . . . is pretty much the same as the sophism of Protagoras, that everything is relative."[64] The society that becomes its own point of reference absolutizes itself; but at the same time it makes everything relative by denying that there is anything outside its own historically particular status quo to which either the individual or the social order is responsible. Within this framework there is the ethics of socialization by which the individual learns to subordinate instinct and private interest to social requirements. But Eichmann and Mengele were good Germans in this sense, and apartheid is what the age demands for Afrikaners. This is why Johannes says the system has no ethics.

The other major cultural embodiment of objectivity in Kierkegaard's world is religious orthodoxy. Whereas the system presupposes faith in its reading public without any questions asked at all,[65] the church is a bit more demanding. It asks the following questions: Do you assent to the propositions that express the content of the Christian faith? and, Have you been baptized? Johannes has no desire to deny that Christianity has an intellectual content that distinguishes it from other religions (and specifically from Hegelian philosophy) nor to affirm that baptism is unimportant or merely optional for Christians. But he vigorously denies that Christianity is simply a doctrine, that faith consists in learning and reciting its content by rote. And he likewise refuses to identify faith with a condition of baptism. For truth in the ethicoreligious sense is inseparable from the inward transformation of the self;[66] and this cannot be identified either with mental assent to propositions or with having had a rite performed on one in the helplessness of infancy. The self, whose subjectivity is ethicoreligious inwardness, may be entirely uninvolved in these intellectual and ritual acts, which simply means that orthodoxy, like speculative philosophy and the aesthetic sphere, is morally neutral.[67]

---

[62]*CUP*, 184-201.

[63]Ibid., 113, 138, 308-309, 123, 129, 309, 427-28.

[64]Ibid., 34n.

[65]Ibid., 18.

[66]Ibid., 61, 68, 192-93, 290-91, 339-40, 537, 325, 333, 539, 37-38.

[67]No doubt this explains how orthodoxy has so often been the historical partner of immorality and atrocity.

This is why Johannes insists that truth is subjectivity and why he suggests that there is more truth in the member of an idolatrous community who prays rightly to the wrong god than in a member of Christendom who prays wrongly to the right God.[68]

For ideological purposes speculative philosophy and Christian orthodoxy are an unbeatable pair. Both interpret the life of spirit in the categories of objectivity, leaving their followers free to shape their lives in terms of one or more of the many, available amoral rationalities—philosophical, religious, political, scientific-technical, and so forth. At the same they hide all this from their followers by reinforcing their self-understanding as members of a Christian nation. The system and the church together create a cultural context in which it is socially in bad taste to ask whether any particular person, including oneself, is a Christian[69] and conceptually incoherent to challenge socially prevalent norms. Individual and society receive the moral and religious sanction that comes with the name Christian, while at the same time they are exempted from the fear and trembling involved in actually living before God.

Johannes speaks, if we will let him, directly to us today. Our situation is not as different from his as might at first appear. Though contemporary America is more secular than Kierkegaard's Denmark, there are loud voices, not without political and economic clout, seeking to "resacralize" American society, to "reclaim its rightful heritage as a Christian nation." While those voices are critical of the instrumental-decisionist rationality that underlies our new national policy on abortion, they aggressively seek to baptize a *raison d'etat* politics and a growth-and-profit economics whose rationality has the same end-justifies-the-means structure as the pro-choice position they decry as secular humanism. Kierkegaard can help us to see how easily the amoral rationality of secular humanism can be incorporated into what presents itself to the world and to itself as Christian. Or, to take another example, when one of the most popular television preachers of our time tells us that repentance is an outmoded category and that the best way to introduce unbelievers to the Christian faith is to avoid talking about sin, we might recognize, with Johannes's help, the ideological character of this preaching, which seeks to eliminate the offense from Jesus' message that one must first repent and then believe the gospel.

On the secular front, our society is not so much under the spell of speculative philosophy as it is under the spell of a scientific-technical rationality whose instrumental-decisionist character plainly represents the triumph of objectivity over the categories of subjectivity.[70] From the point of view of eth-

---

[68]*CUP*, 179-81.

[69]Ibid., 19, 49, 181n.

[70]This is true even in positivism and some forms of existentialism where emphasis is placed on the decisionist dimension. The arbitrary choice this involves can be called subjectivity only in a sense that is nearly opposite Johannes's definition.

ics and religion, the differences between the world of the system and the world of the expert are not as important as their common ground. So while it would be hard to find many adherents of Hegel's philosophy of world history as such, we nonetheless believe that our form of society—democratic, capitalist, and scientific—is the goal of human history: the last, best hope of the world. And our preoccupation with the world stage on which the super powers play out their arrogance and insecurity is not so very different from the historicist spectatorism with which Johannes was acquainted.

So the untimely meditations of Johannes Climacus are timely after all. Perhaps there will always be those who dismiss him and Kierkegaard, who stands behind him, as irrationalists because they are insufficiently reverent toward the amoral rationality and inoffensive piety that modernity calls Reason. We would do well to remember that Socrates and the early Christians were accused of atheism because they did not worship at the shrines of the self-absolutizing cultures in which they lived.

Index